CROSS STITCH
DESIGN MANUAL

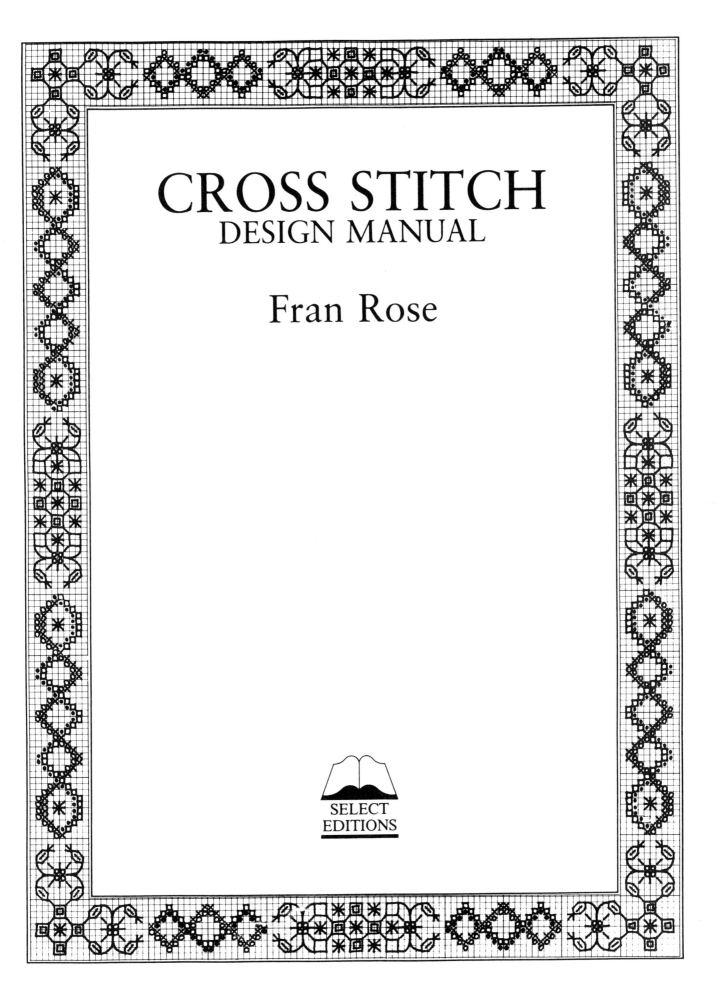

CROSS STITCH
DESIGN MANUAL

Fran Rose

SELECT
EDITIONS

ISBN 1 85648 196 4

First published 1987
Second impression 1988
Third impression 1988
Fourth impression 1988

This edition published 1994 by
The Promotional Reprint Company
exclusively for Selecta Books Limited,
Roundway, Devizes, UK

Printed in Malaysia

Contents

Introduction

The aim of this book is to give the beginner the basic skills of cross stitch and to offer to the more experienced needleworker a structured approach to designing original work. It can be worked through systematically or just 'dipped' into. The ideas contained in the book will, I hope, stimulate you to have a go for yourself. I find that my 'hobby' cannot be divorced from the daily pattern of my life and find myself constantly looking almost unconsciously for new ideas. 'No sense of proportion!' my husband would say! You cannot separate yourself from the past and its influences either, so you must build on them and create your own contribution.

The background to my work is difficult to define. I suppose I am always looking at things afresh and reassessing myself; such is the nature of teaching, and I have taught both children and adults for twenty years. This is the most important feature – to pass on one's own ideas and skills. My childhood surrounded me with beautiful things – my aunt who made lovely clothes for people and my mother who opened my eyes to the beauty of our national heritage and encouraged me to develop an interest in music, dance and drama.

It was not until I came to Norfolk that I was able to devote more time to my craft and I am grateful for the stimulation that the countryside gave me and the support and encouragement given to me by the many talented craftworkers I have met here. They – and my students too – have taught me to develop my skills more fully.

I always say to a group of students when they embark on a new craft that their lives will never be the same again – you have been warned!

The ideas and designs throughout the book are largely taken direct from my own design manual and show how I go about my work. I make a point of recording the details of colours and materials directly on to the charts for future reference, often noting the time taken to stitch them and the date too. It is always interesting to look back through the charts in my portfolio to see how trends have developed, particularly since many of the completed embroideries will have been given away or sold.

1
Getting Started

The first effective way of linking pieces of skin or fabric together was lacing and from this crossing over of threads we can trace the origins of cross stitch, which came into particular prominence in eighteenth- and nineteenth-century samplers. In fact it is sometimes known as sampler stitch or as marking stitch because it was frequently employed to mark initials on household linen.

This book sets out to provide a working manual that takes full account of the important influences of the past and gives practical help and encouragement to those who wish to design their own pieces and be as inventive as their predecessors. I delight in using the patterns and stitches that have satisfied embroiderers for hundreds of years. They utilised designs, materials and stitches to suit their own needs and so indeed should we.

Whatever work we do, it must be our best. It is important to aim for the highest standards from the very beginning. Our work reflects us and we will want to be able to appreciate it for many years to come, so it will pay to use materials of good quality. Time and trouble spent in choosing the right threads and fabrics will help us to avoid problems and frustrations as the work progresses.

Cross stitch is a counted thread process and requires an evenly woven fabric. If you use inferior threads or cloth it will show. Call in at your local craft shop and see the full range of materials available. While there, look at the frames too. I think it is essential to use a frame to keep your work clean and square. You can try working without one but you will soon see why most embroiderers have a selection of frames and USE them.

Fabrics

Evenweave fabrics are available from 10# to 36# (this means from 10 to 36 holes *or* threads to the inch) and you need to choose a density that will suit the design you have planned, the required finished dimensions of the work and your eyesight. A hole means the space between the warp and weft threads of the fabric through which you pass your needle. There are many different weights and qualities of fabric available in various natural shades and also in different colours. Aida, Glenshee and Hardanger are all cottons and there is also a range of linens. They come in a variety of widths from 3in (8cm) to 48in (122cm). Some have dressing in them and may become limp after working. Pressing with a steam iron on the back will stiffen them and help to straighten them too if necessary. Perforated paper is also suitable; more details on this may be found in Chapter 6.

Threads

Threads are available in a bewildering variety. Designs in this book have been worked singly or in a combination of the following: stranded cottons, perlé, silk, coton à broder, polyester, and gold and silver threads. Remember that threads vary in thickness. As a general rule the thread must pass through the fabric without causing any distortion. Often two or more stitches may pass through the same hole, so allow for this.

The following list suggests the best use for different threads according to the coarseness of the evenweave fabric:

Stranded cottons – 6 strands	10–15 use 3 strands 15–26 use 2 strands 26+ use 1 strand
Coton à broder – single thread	10–26; may be too thick beyond this
Crochet cotton	10–20
Commercial glitter	These come in a variety of thicknesses
Danish flower threads	10–20 use 2 strands 20+ use 1 strand
Cotton perlé	Suitable for coarser fabrics
Silk	Suitable for very fine work – take care as the dyes can leave colour behind, so there is no room for mistakes

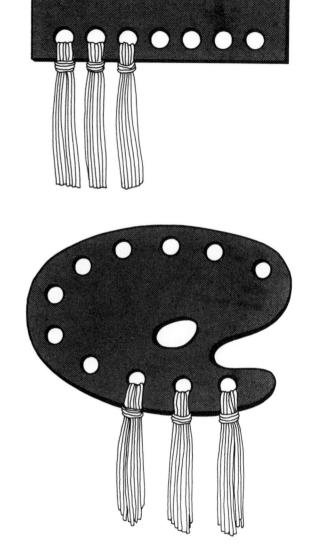

Choosing your colours

The choice of colour is important. Make your choice in daylight as artificial light can distort the tones and shades. Colours will appear lighter on your work than in the skein, particularly when using stranded threads. If you divide six strands into three pairs, the colour will be paler. What you choose is up to you and it must please you. Making decisions about which colours blend well together is a very individual process. For the absolute beginner one way is to take one colour and work through its tonal shades, or to limit your work to three contrasting colours. If you know where the work is destined to be displayed you can select colours that will harmonize with those already in use there. I have a great love of black – it gives such a good definition of line and will fit in with such a variety of other colours. Nature combines colours quite successfully! Seasonal colours are a good guide, as is actually analysing how many different colours go to make a rose or a sunset. Train your eyes to look and see.

Thread palettes (Fig 1)

The usual working length of threads is 12–15 in (30–37.5 cm); any longer and they will fray, break, tangle or get grubby. Make a cardboard palette to hold your colours by punching holes in a strip of cardboard and tying the threads with a lark's head knot through the holes. Alternatively, make an artist's palette from plywood, particularly useful when working with wools.

Fig 1 Keep threads and wools in good order on a cardboard or wooden palette

Put the colours in a working order that you will remember. This is useful at night when artificial light can be deceiving.

Needles

The needles used are blunt tapestry needles. They come in a range of sizes from 18 to 24; the higher the number the finer the needle. It should pass through the hole in the fabric without disturbing the weave of the cloth. Always keep your needles somewhere dry so they do not rust. When you leave your work remember to thread the needle into the material and not leave it hanging or you *will* lose it!

Frames

Depending on the size of the piece you are sewing you will need a different size of frame. There are two basic types – rings and rollers. Ring frames begin at about 4in (10cm) in diameter and go up to quilting frames, often on stands, of 24in (60cm) diameter. They should be bound with white tape to help prevent marking your fabric. However, I have found that even taking great care there is often a shadow mark left by the ring which does not come out even after washing and ironing, so I always try to complete my work and allow for mounting within the confines of the ring. Using a roller frame means that you can set up a long length of fabric to do large projects or several smaller ones.

Setting up a ring frame (Fig 2)

Cut the fabric at least 2½in (12cm) larger all round than the size of the outer frame. You can cut a square of material if you like and whip-stitch the edges or tape them with masking tape. Lay your outer ring – with the screw loosened – flat on the table, then lay your fabric right side down over the ring. Next push the inner ring down firmly to trap the fabric between the two rings. Turn the frame over and make sure the screw is at the top of your work so you will not catch your threads in it. Check the fabric is square and even in the frame, easing where

necessary. Finally tighten the screw; you are aiming for drum tightness. Now your ring is ready. I often set up several at once so there is always one ready to use.

Setting up a roller frame (Fig 3)

Cut your fabric 1in (2.5cm) narrower than the width of the roller. Turn the sides of the fabric in ½in (1.25cm) and tack along the length. Do the same at the top and bottom. You may prefer to tape the edges with masking tape; if so, make your fabric 2in (5cm) narrower than the width of the roller. Pin top and bottom to the fabric on the rollers and then tack in place with strong thread. Finish off well and tie a knot so that the fabric will not pull off when it is under tension. Tighten the wing nuts on the top roller and roll the fabric onto the other end until it is taut. Now tighten the wing nuts at that end. Lace the sides as shown in Fig 3. You will need to release this lacing and relace your work when you roll on.

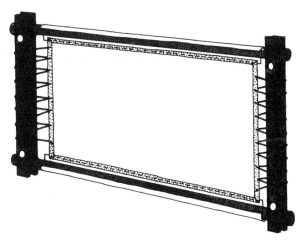

Fig 3 Setting up a roller frame

Graph paper

To plot your own designs you will need graph paper. Black is best if you intend to photocopy your design to pass it on to a friend. This can be bought from stationers in both metric and imperial sizes, either in small pads or large sheets. You will also need sharp pencils with a soft lead, a good soft rubber and a fine black felt-tipped pen. It is useful to keep large sheets in cardboard rolls such as the inner tubes of cooking foil.

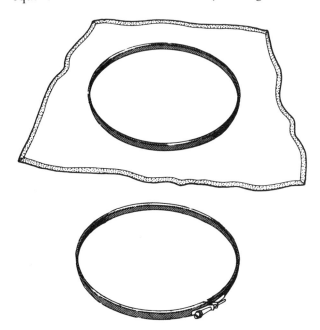

Fig 2 Setting up a ring frame

How to read patterns

If you are going to read someone else's pattern you must familiarise yourself with it before you start. First find the centre, mark top and bottom and side to side, then make a grid. You may find it useful to mark in the colours with felt-tipped pens or crayons, but do be careful to keep them away from your work. It is all too easy to leave the tops off . . .

Fig 4 In this example, stitching was started at the 'c' of cloud by counting down from the centre top; alternatively, it could have been started at the 'E' of every

Where to start

It is always difficult to decide where to begin as each piece could be stitched in a variety of ways. With the motto designs in this book, the letters were usually stitched first beginning at the top centre, working first to the right and then back from the centre to the left. Check and count several times to be sure before you begin (Fig 4). The border and pictorial work come next (Fig 5). If the chart is densely covered it is useful to mark out the length of the lines and gaps before you start. Put your chart in a polybag or plastic sleeve, then you can mark off as you go and your chart will not be spoiled.

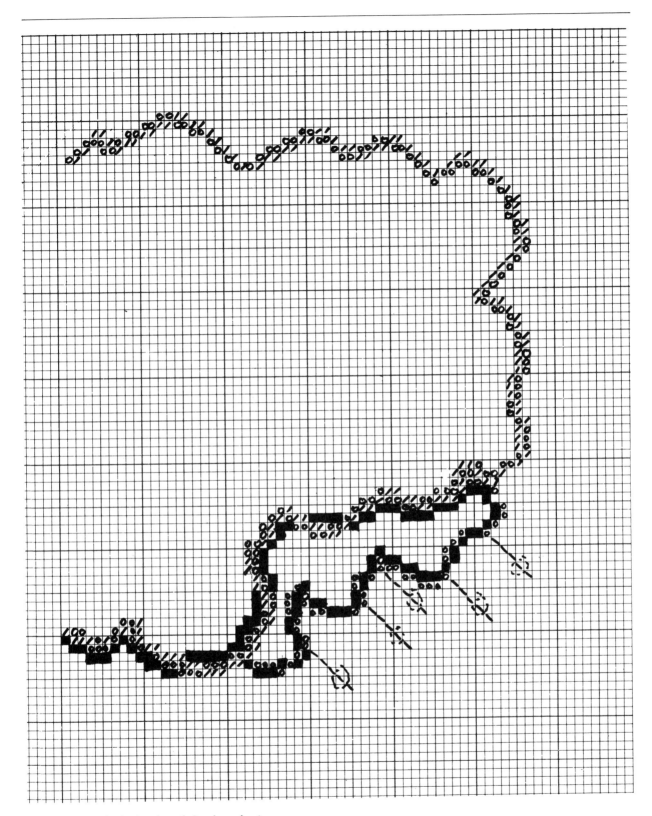

Fig 5 Now work the border of clouds and rain

A
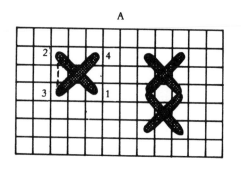

B
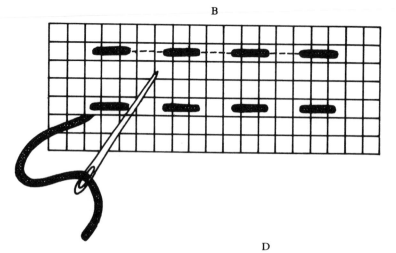

C
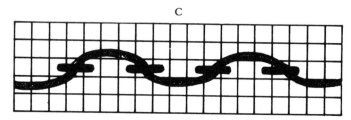

D
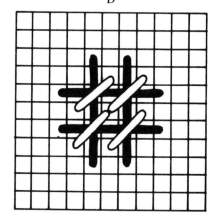

E
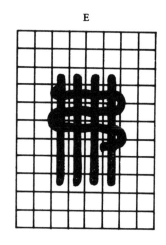

F
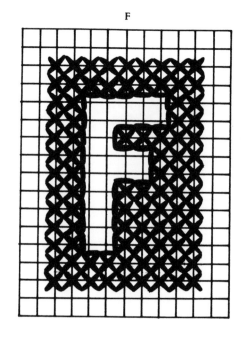

G
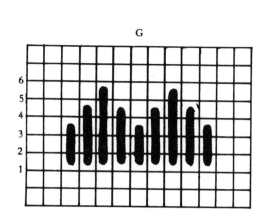

Fig 6 Stitches used in this book

A Cross stitch Follow the numbers to work the cross; each cross should lie the same way and one hole is common to both crosses

B Double running stitch Stitch over three holes and under three holes, then go back and fill in the gaps; this stitch is similar to back stitch but uses less thread and the back is less bulky

C Weaving Work a running stitch through alternate holes, then weave a contrast thread through on the surface

D Couching Stitch a grid, first of vertical lines, then of horizontal lines; catch them down together with a diagonal stitch over three holes in a contrast colour

E Needleweaving Work long stitches vertically, then weave in and out until the vertical threads are covered

F Assisi The design is left unstitched while the background is completely made up of crosses; the design is then outlined in double running stitch

G Florentine or Bargello Work vertical stitches side by side varying in length to form a pattern

How to stitch

You must be comfortable, warm (fingers get cold quickly) and sit in a good light. Daylight, particularly early morning, is best. If you have to work in artificial light, invest in a good anglepoise lamp; some are available with a magnifier. If you are working on a hand roller frame, rest it between a table and your lap to leave your hands free. Floor frames are available and make a good Christmas present for the serious worker. Have all you need ready before you start:

> small scissors or snips
> spare needles pinned into fabric
> threads arranged on a palette or tied onto roller frame
> pattern

Tack the grid marked on your pattern in white thread with large stitches.

Now start working the design, using A (Fig 6) for the lettering and B–F (Fig 6) for pictorial work.

Remember, there should not be any knots; darn in ends at the back to give a neat finish. Do not trail your threads from one letter to another as some fabrics are not densely woven and the threads will show through.

Finishing

Remove your work from the frame. If it is grubby give it a gentle hand wash; let it dry naturally and press it lightly on the back before you mount it or make it up. Otherwise just press it gently on the back with a steam iron.

Mounting on a card

Cut the card to the right size. Allow a border on your fabric of 2in (5cm) all round. Mark the centre top and bottom on the card and fabric. Put clear adhesive around the edge of the card. Centre your work over the card and press into place. Ease out any wrinkles and check that it is straight. Trim away any excess fabric with sharp scissors.

A good framer will turn your work into a masterpiece. The mount and frame are very important so have large pieces done professionally if you can afford to do so. A mount and a frame in a sympathetic colour will enhance your design. Small projects can be mounted and framed in purchased frames quite successfully and instructions are given in Chapter 6.

Do's and don'ts

DO keep a notebook for ideas, colour orders and special threads.

DO keep one ring frame ready to try out new stitches and colour combinations.

DO keep a folder later on when you have lots of samples – it looks most impressive. It was from my folders and teaching notes that this book came about.

DO buy enough thread to complete your project as dye lots vary.

DO stitch a line of crosses until your thread is used up. This will give you a rough guide to estimate how much thread you will need.

DON'T strain your eyes. Do a little stitching at a time. Use a magnifier if you need to. I have a pair of glasses which magnify – not flattering but they save headaches!

DON'T leave your work lying around – cats like to sleep on fine work. Put it away in a bag – or a pillowcase for large pieces.

2
Calligraphic Cross Stitch

Calligraphy means beautiful writing and if you have tried it with a pen or brush you will know how hard it is to keep your letters regular in height and width. The spacing between the letters makes a tremendous difference to the effect of the finished result.

With cross stitch on evenweave fabric most of these problems are solved for you. Because each letter is stitched over a counted number of holes, the height and width are determined by the evenness of the material. This leaves you to complete the task by ensuring you sew with a consistent tension, not too loose or too tight, which sits neatly on the surface of the fabric. You will be delighted by the regularity of the script even if it takes longer to complete than writing with a pen. Spacing is automatic because you always leave the same number of holes between each letter. In calligraphy on paper, each space must be calculated by eye; in fact, the intervals that are left are quite deliberately not always the same. You cannot do this with cross stitch but it is a small price to pay when compared with the near-perfect lettering you can so quickly learn to produce.

The alphabets

Study the alphabets in this chapter (Figs 7–12). Some are taken from early samplers and others are original. Each one uses a specific unit of height and width although some have ascenders

and descenders and some use more than one unit in width. When you plan out a motto you wish to sew, you must first calculate the number of holes you will be covering so that the finished phrase will fit exactly where you want it to.

These letters will usually take up one unit of height and width

a c e n o r s u v x z

These letters go higher or lower but keep the same width

b d f g h j k l p q t y

These letters are wider

m w

The letter i like the letters l and j can sometimes be a single stroke, or curves can be added to make them the same unit width. Serifs, the little hooks sometimes added to lettering, can be used. It is best to be consistent with them. Numbers and capital letters again conform to the same pattern.

In many samplers worked by young girls and some boys in the past there was a tremendous amount of counting. They usually worked from a stitched sample and not a pattern draft. When you think that some were only five or six years old it is hardly surprising that they sometimes made mistakes. The chart for a sampler worked by Maryann Kemp in 1816 is shown as Fig 107 in Chapter 7.

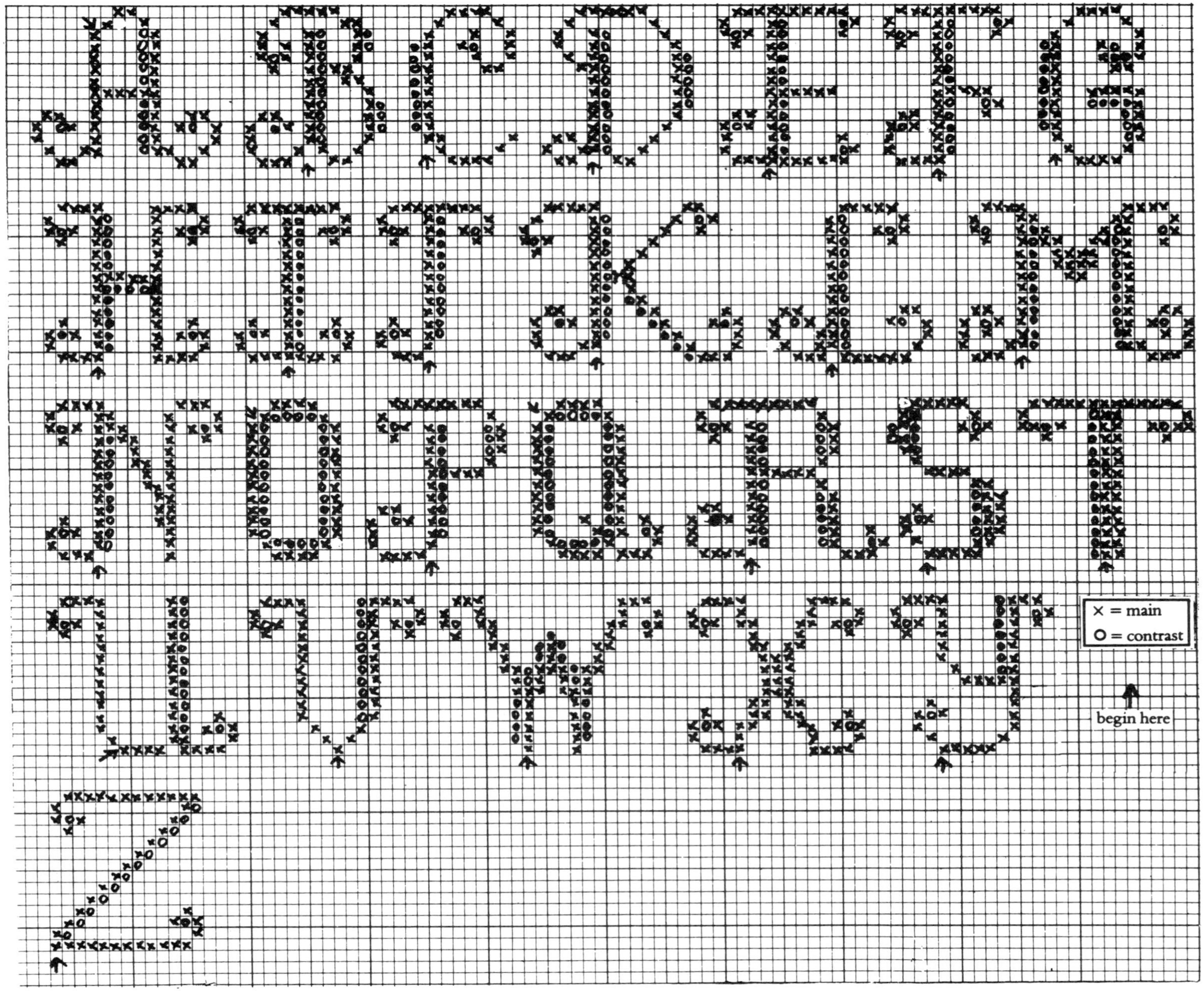

Fig 7

X = main
O = contrast

← begin here

Fig 8

A range of evenweave fabrics and perforated paper

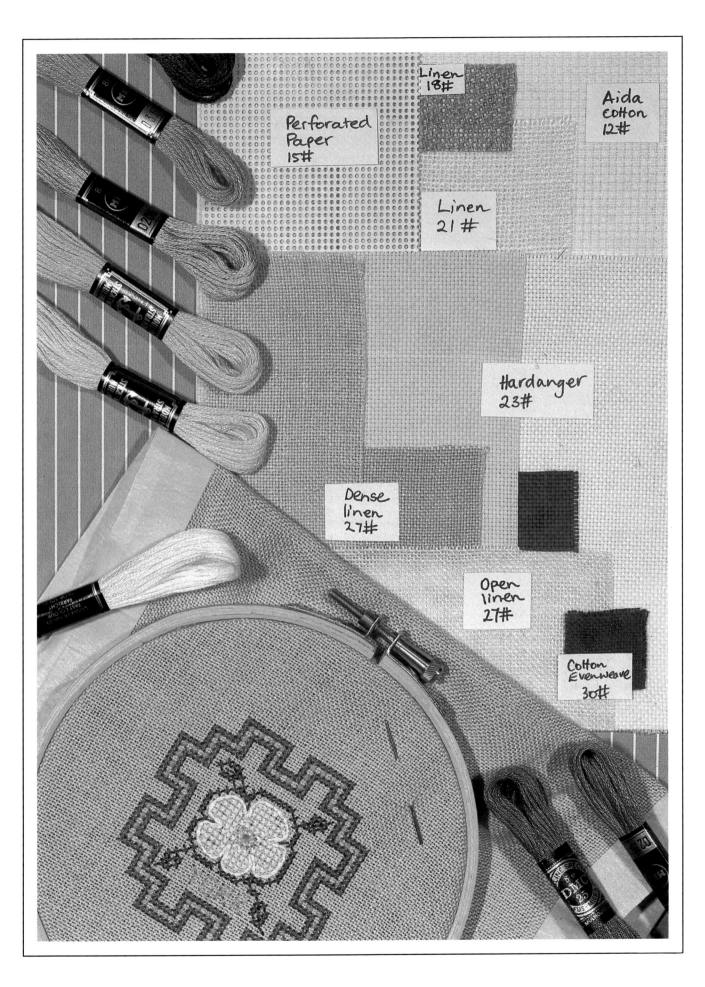

Perforated
Paper
15#

Linen
18#

Aida
cotton
12#

Linen
21 #

Hardanger
23#

Dense
linen
27#

Open
linen
27#

Cotton
Evenweave
30#

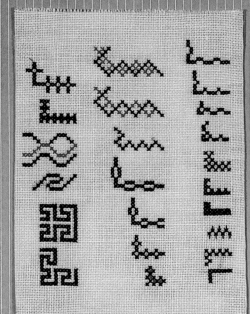

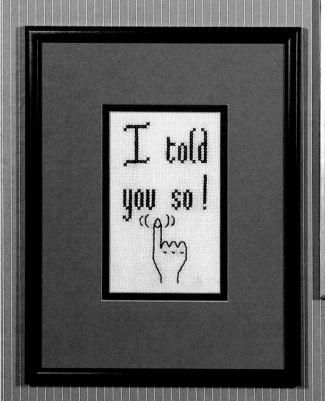

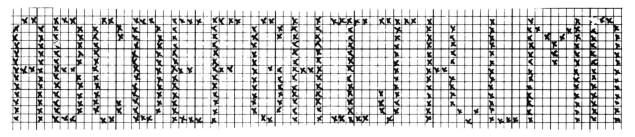

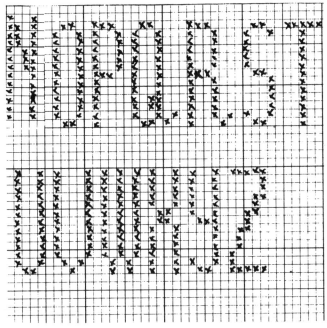

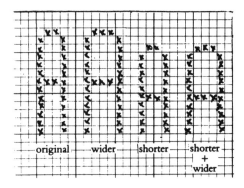

original — wider — shorter — shorter + wider

Fig 9 Alphabet 13 high by 4, 5, 6 or 7 wide; if reduced to 11 high this alphabet links well with lower case 5 high. The width and height can be varied as shown

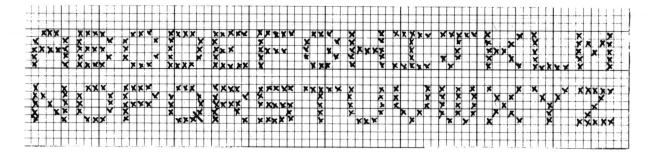

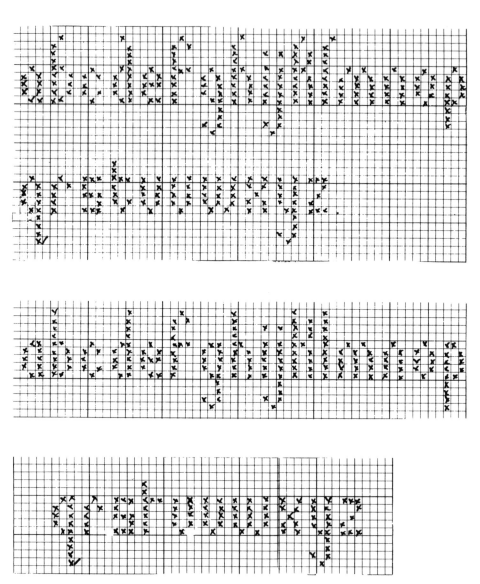

Fig 10 Alphabet of capitals built on 5 by 5 crosses, with lower case built on 5 high by 3 across with 4 for the curved descenders, also showing a variation with straight descenders

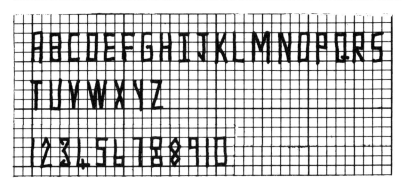

Fig 11 Alphabet using double running stitch, 7 high by 3
wide, useful for small initials inside hearts etc where space
is limited

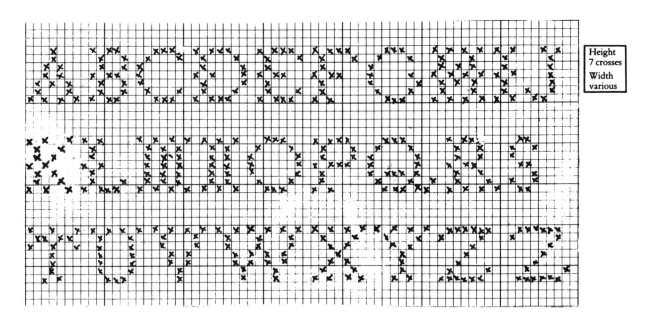

Height
7 crosses

Width
various

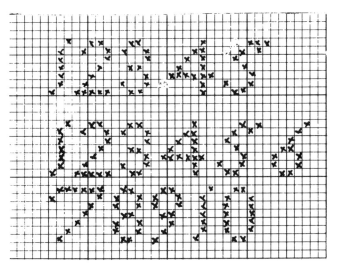

Fig 12 Alphabet of capitals, numerals and lower case from
the Maryann Kemp sampler

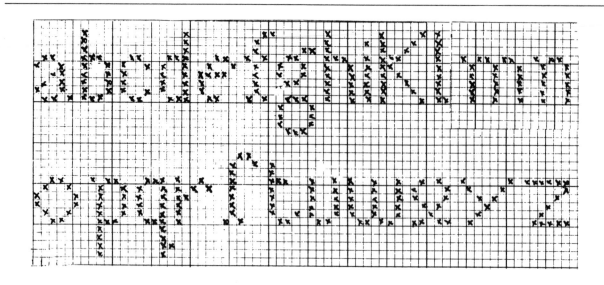

A small project to begin with

Start by stitching your own initial. Choose a capital from one of the alphabets and plot it out on graph paper. Remember to mark the centre on your graph and count your holes. Now stitch it centrally on your fabric. Next, look at the borders in Chapter 3. Count out an equal number of holes on all sides and then plot your border. Keep it simple this time – a single line or parallel lines will be fine.

Fig 13 shows five examples worked out by one of my students. Most of the designs in this book have been tested out by beginners and those with up to three years' experience.

a) This is a simple design broken at the corner. With mainly straight lines it is easy to follow (120 stitches).

b) There is a lot more stitching here (245 stitches). The idea was to complement the heavy Y with a dense border leaving the gaps on each side to create interest.

c) The Z seemed a bit stark in a simple square frame but looks more comfortable with the extra squares in the corners.

d) The corners of the diagonally placed square border are emphasised by the two extra stitches and the four balls in the corners help to give stability to the design.

e) The more florid K demanded a border in sympathy with it. Perhaps it could have been less angular and more curved?

These one-off initials, because they do not have to fit in with other letters, can be designed individually. You will find that the examples do not exactly match the alphabets given.

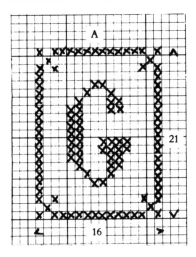

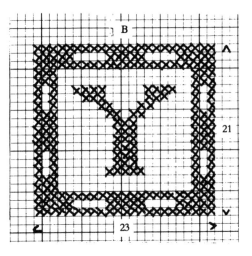

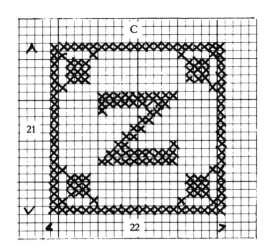

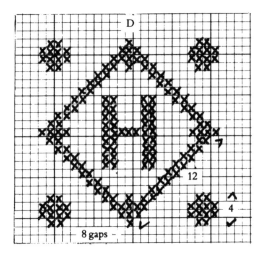

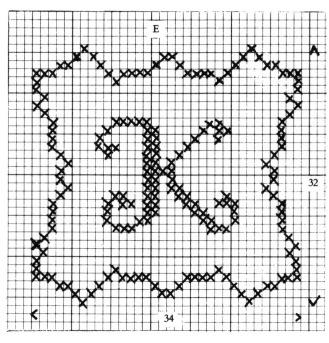

Fig 13 Decorated initials

Mottoes and sayings

Now why not try something more complicated? Mottoes and short rhymes are great fun to do. These can range from a single word like 'Mañana' (Spanish for 'don't let's bother with it today – wait till tomorrow) to quite lengthy pieces of work.

You may want to illustrate some aspect of the idea being worked or relate the border – if you have one – to it. Here are some phrases and sayings you might like to choose from, but of course you'll enjoy it even more if you choose some favourite quip of your own.

one word
Toujours
Mañana
Names
Initials

two words
Sweet Dreams
Be Mine
Forever Yours
Je t'aime
Remember Me

three words
Be My Guest
C'est la Vie
God is Love
Home Sweet Home
Forget-Me-Not
Bless This House
Spring is Sprung
Nostalgia rules O.K.
Toujours l'Amour
Count Your Blessings

four words
Be of Good Cheer
In God We Trust
Be Gone Dull Care
Health Wealth and Happiness

five words
Kissing Don't Last – Cookery Do
Memories give Roses in December
While There's Tea There's Hope
Everyman Paddle his own Canoe
Come you in my Beauty
All's Well That Ends Well

six words
Every Cloud Has A Silver Lining
To Thine Own Self Be True
Bien Mangé, Bien Bu, Merci Jésus
Si jeunesse savait – Si vieillesse pouvait
There's No Place Like Home
Humpty Dumpty Sat On A Wall

seven or more words
So Little Done – So Much To Do
He Loves Me – He Loves Me Not
Some Folks Are Wise And Some Are Otherwise
Men Are But Children Of A Larger Growth
Kind Words Are The Music Of the World
Je t'aime Aujourd'hui Un Peu Plus Qu'hier Mais Bien Moins Que Demain

Remember how long the initial took you to do, so you will be able to estimate how long to allow for a motto. Here is how I worked out the exhortation 'Be Mine' one February some years ago.

Using Alphabet B and allowing 1 space (1 hole) between letters and 5 spaces (5 holes) between words, I wrote it out like this (Fig 14):

Fig 14

I counted the total number of holes required which was 61, arrived at by counting the stitches and gaps, multiplying by 2 and adding 1. This is because each cross shares a common hole with the next one. So if your cross is 3×3 and there are 30 stitches, you will have 30×2+1=61 holes. If your cross is 4×4 holes and you have 30

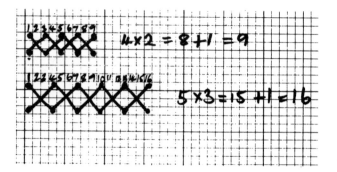

Fig 15

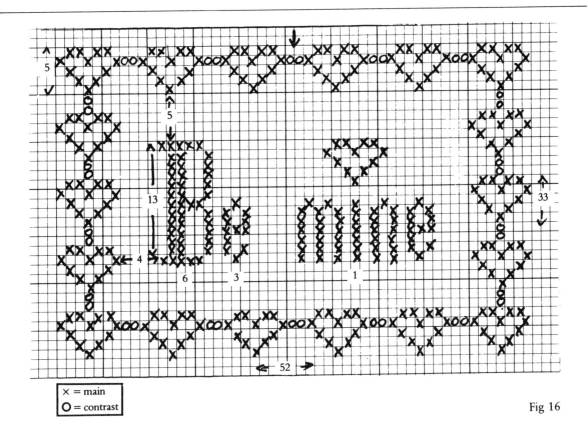

× = main
O = contrast

Fig 16

stitches, you will need 30×3+1=91 holes. Your design will work out much bigger, as shown in Fig 15.

The tallest letter in 'Be mine' is the capital B which is 13 stitches high requiring 27 holes. I then made sure that my fabric was big enough to accommodate 61×27 holes plus room for the border of hearts to go round it. The completed charted design is shown in Fig 16.

To make them fit round easily, I worked out that, as each heart had a width of 7 stitches, I could fit 6 across leaving a gap of 4 stitches width on either side between the hearts and words. I needed a gap of 5 stitches to accommodate 5 hearts placed down the sides. All this allowed for a linking rope of a contrasting colour – two stitches between each heart. As there was a large gap above 'mine' because it was stitched in lower case letters with no ascenders, it seemed obvious to replace the dot of the i with a heart; in fact, as well as balancing up the right hand side of the design, there is also the little accidental symbolism of 'I give my heart'.

Blocking a longer motto

Sometimes you may want to block a motto into a space so that each line begins and ends at the same place vertically. 'Be gone dull care' is an example of blocking a motto into a design.

Having counted up the stitches for each word, I decided upon a line length that would provide me with acceptable central gaps (Fig 17). Then I plotted from the extreme left of the line for 'Be' and 'dull' and backwards from the extreme right for 'gone' and 'care'.

This time I decided on a more pictorial approach to the border with the sun breaking through between the clouds above and a flower border at the base. The finished chart is shown in Fig 18.

By now you will be finding it easier to read charts and to begin to design for yourself. On the following pages are designs I have worked with just a few comments here and there. Feel free to copy them, but I would like to think you will now have enough confidence to make up your own.

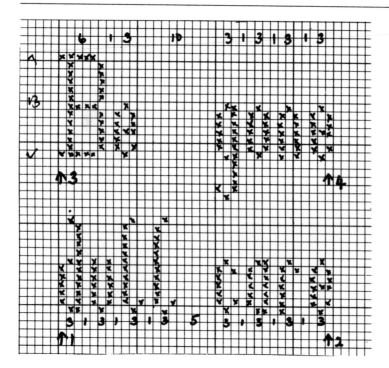

Fig 17

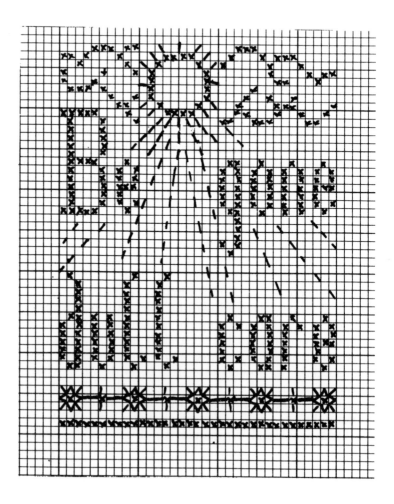

Fig 18

| × = 3 x 3 holes incl |
| Hardanger fabric |
| × = dark |
| O = contrast |
| ⊔⊔⊔ = contrast |
| ⊠ = dark |

Fig 19

Fig 20

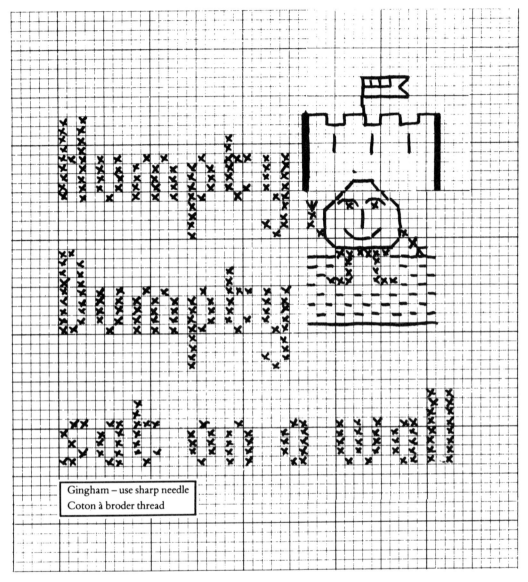

Fig 21

× = 3 x 3 holes incl
Hessian **#** or Hardanger
× = brown
O = blue

Fig 22

centre

one hole gap between

× = 3 x 3 holes incl
Fine linen 30 **#**
Stranded cotton, 2 threads
× = green
— = green
O = blue
3–4 hours

centre

Fig 23

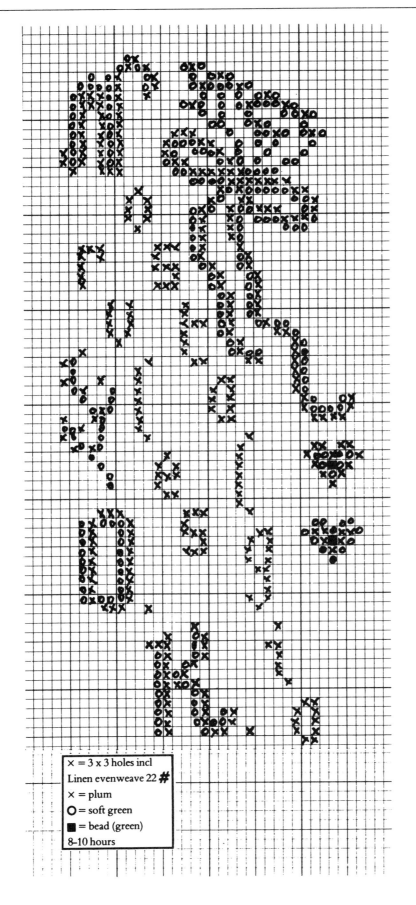

x = 3 x 3 holes incl
Linen evenweave 22 #
x = plum
O = soft green
■ = bead (green)
8–10 hours

Fig 24

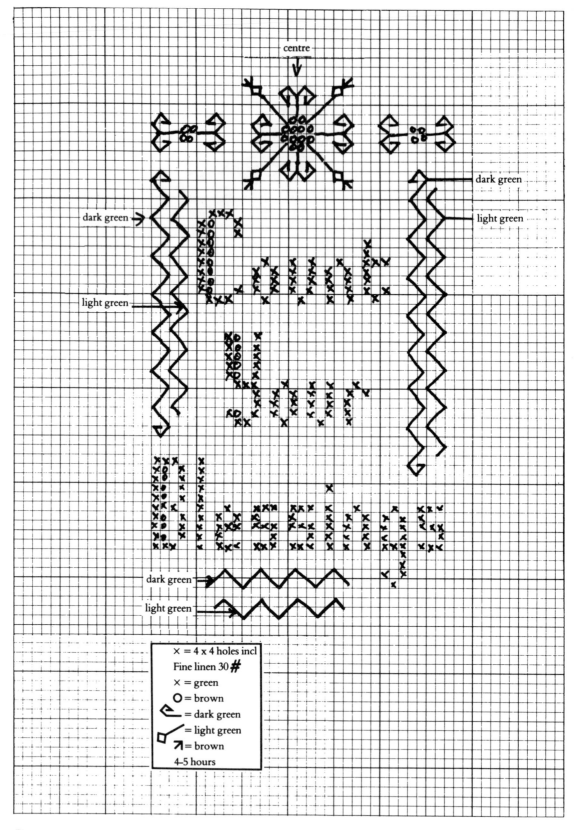

Fig 25

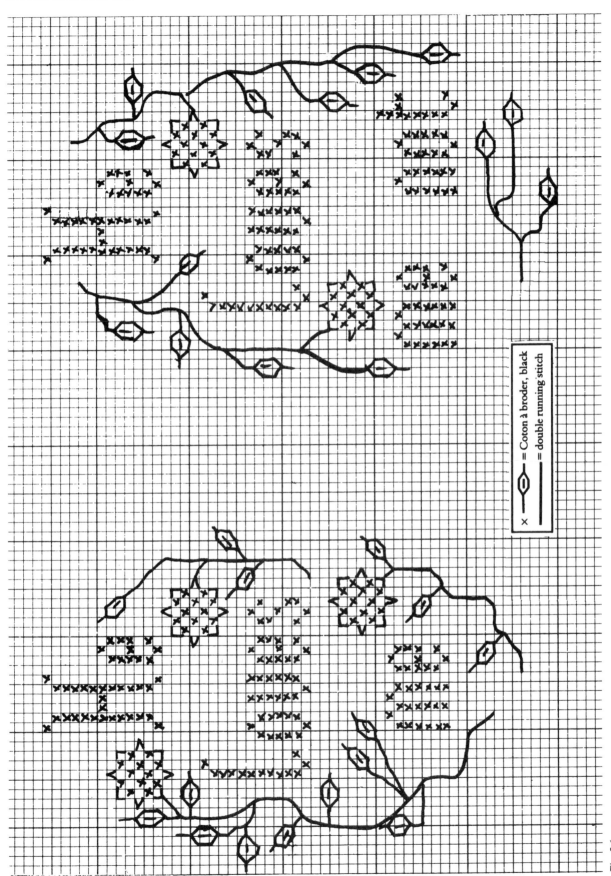

× = Coton à broder, black

= double running stitch

Fig 26

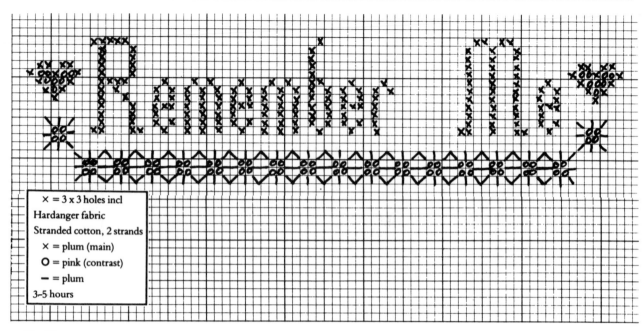

× = 3 x 3 holes incl
Hardanger fabric
Stranded cotton, 2 strands
× = plum (main)
O = pink (contrast)
— = plum
3–5 hours

Fig 27

Linen evenweave 18 **#**
Shaded stranded cotton,
  plum through pink
× = letters = shading
    as it comes
O = pink tones
◇ = double running
    stitch using
    lighter tones
4 hours

Fig 28

Calligraphic cross stitch in a variety of styles (see Figs 4, 21, 26, 30 and 31 for charts)

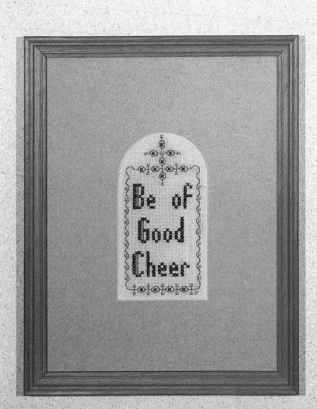

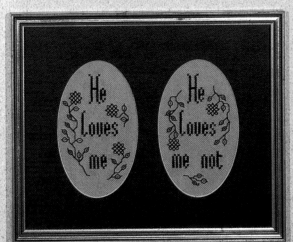

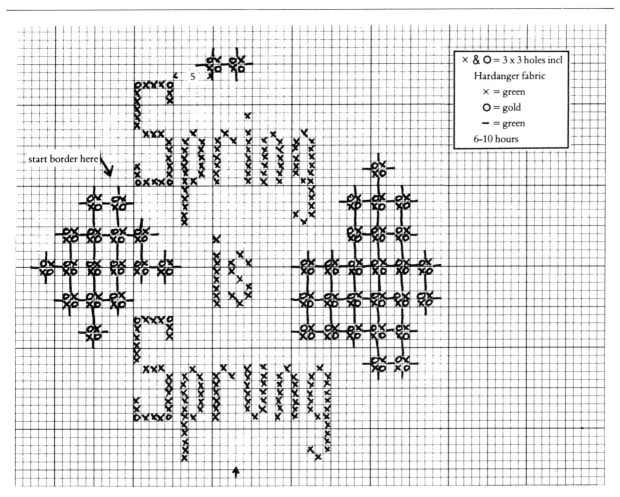

Fig 29

Careful choice of colours and natural wood frames
emphasise the cottage-style of these designs (see Figs 18,
20, 24, 25 and 29 for charts)

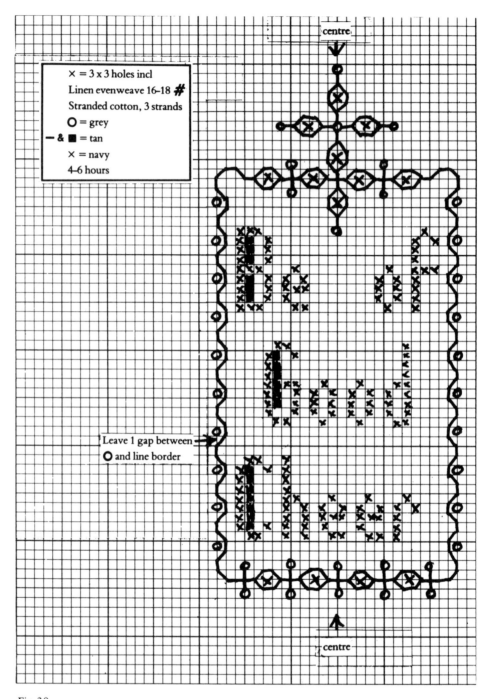

Fig 30

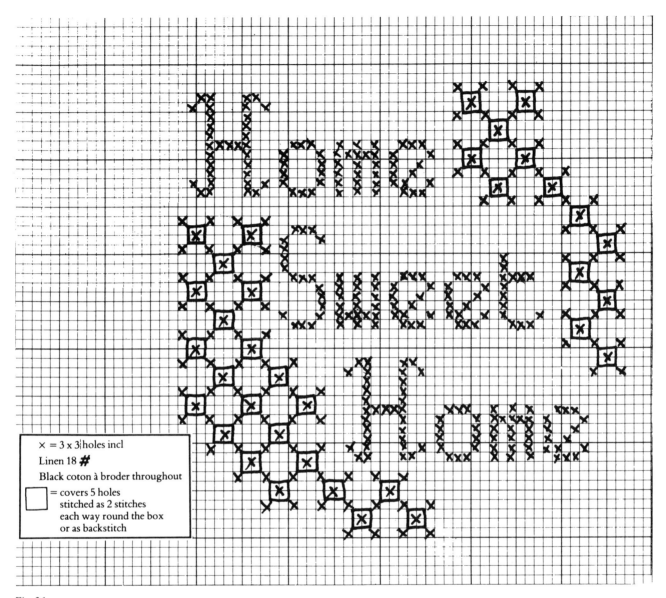

× = 3 x 3 holes incl

Linen 18 **#**

Black coton à broder throughout

☐ = covers 5 holes
stitched as 2 stitches
each way round the box
or as backstitch

Fig 31

centre

Some folks are wise and some are otherwise.

× = 3 x 3 holes incl
Hardanger fabric
Black coton à broder throughout
∧ = double running stitch
8 hours

Fig 32

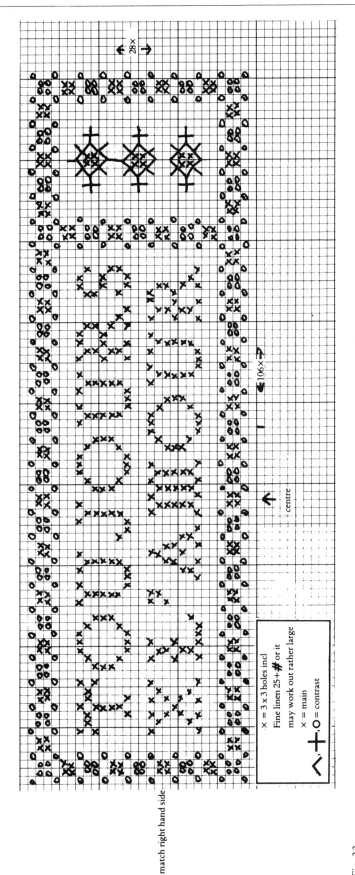

28×

106×

centre

match right hand side

x = 3 x 3 holes incl
Fine linen 25+ # or it
may work out rather large
× = main
‹, o = contrast

Fig 33

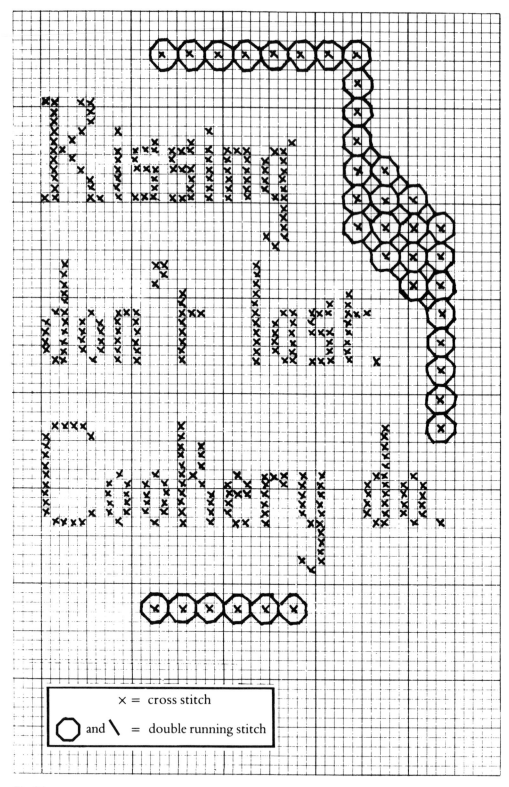

Fig 34

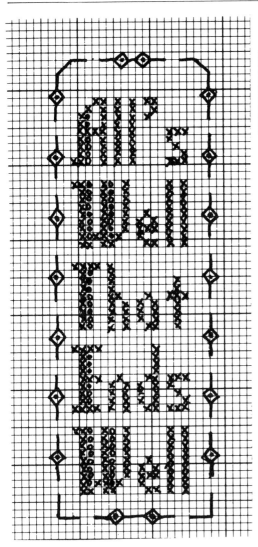

Fig 35

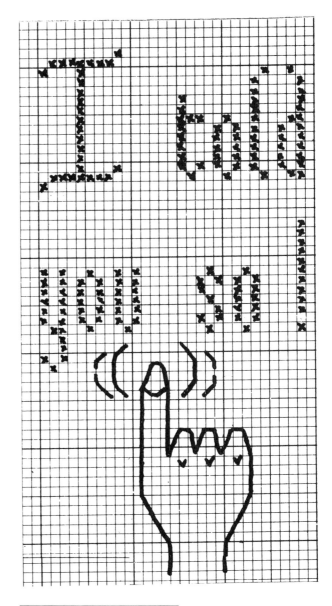

Fig 36

3
Borders and Linked Motifs

Borders always look complicated but if you analyse them they can be simplified down to a small repeat unit. By looking at other samplers and embroideries in museums and by applying a mathematical approach, I have produced a series of borders from a simple straight line to more complex structures (Fig 37). All require accurate planning and execution. In particular, cornering requires accurate counting. If the number of holes does not divide accurately for your chosen border, you may need to add 1 cross at the corner. All the samples shown have a corner worked to help you.

Always centre your work with a tacking thread and work from the centre outwards. These borders can be stitched over either 2, 3 or 4 holes (inclusive) to vary the size.

Combinations of these patterns will give the appearance of a very complicated border; only you will know just how simple it is to produce.

1 This begins as a straight line with a variation of alternate colours, forming a sequential pattern.

2 The pattern alternates 1 up 1 down.

3 By adding a single vertical line dividing the stitch, you can achieve a feathery effect.

4 This double straight line gives a much firmer outline.

5 The first of various permutations of 1 up 2 down, 2 up 1 down, etc.

6–10 The up and down idea is followed through.

11 Building on from this by the addition of a contrast colour, diamonds are created.

12–14 Variations on this.

15 A zigzag pattern to a depth of 3 crosses; try different heights.

16 Two zigzags in contrasting colours are worked to go in opposite directions.

17 Add a third colour and see how the pattern changes.

18 The Greek Key pattern gives a lovely flow – a complete border is given later in Fig 51.

19 A variation on 18.

20 A deep border giving a wave pattern.

21 An undulating pattern.

22 The pattern is repeated with a second colour echoing the first.

23 Two undulating patterns are combined to give irregular hexagons.

24 Extra crosses in the centre again change the balance.

25–26 Developments enlarging patterns vertically.

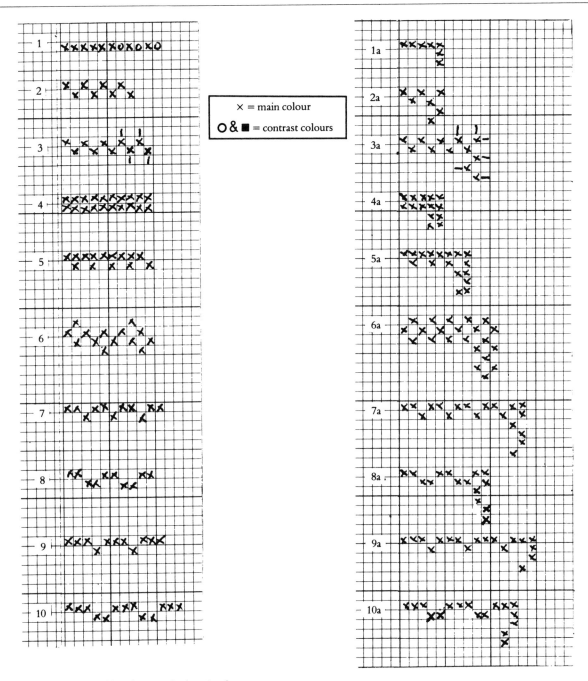

Fig 37a A wide range of borders, each showing how to turn
a corner

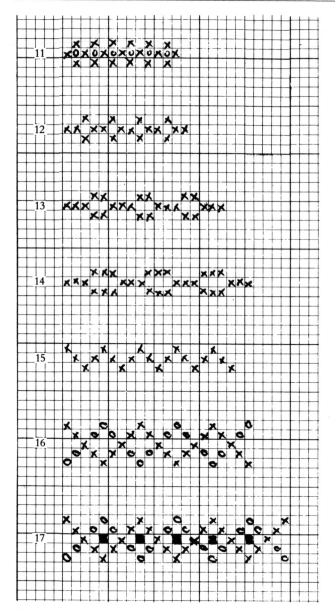

Fig 37b

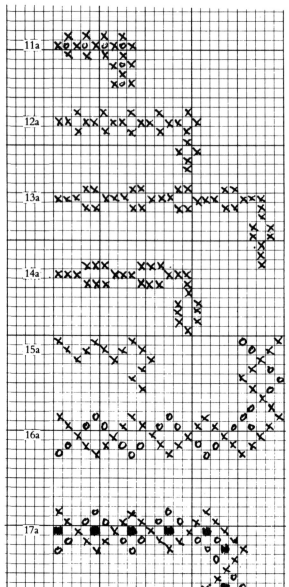

Fig 37c

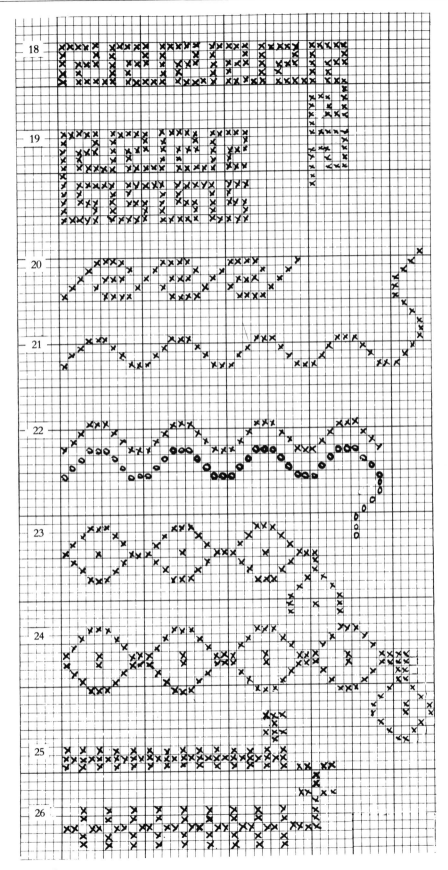

Fig 37d

Linked motifs

Stars and hearts have appeared in cross stitch designs throughout the centuries. Here are some variations of mine. I have given basic star shapes in different sizes (Fig 38) and shown three full borders of stars simply linked together (Figs 39–41). Try filling them in a variety of ways. Star Border 3 combines two stars for a different effect.

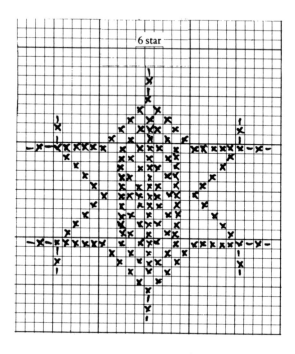

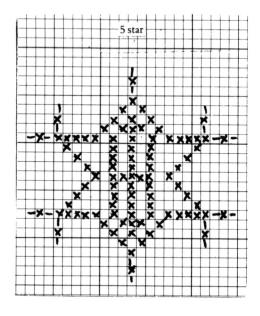

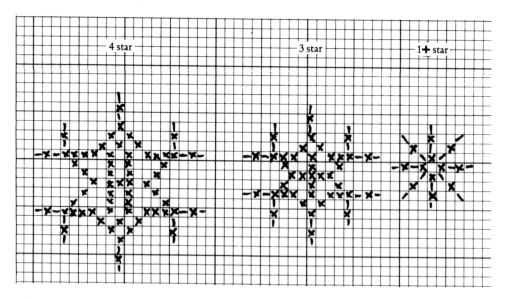

Fig 38 Stars

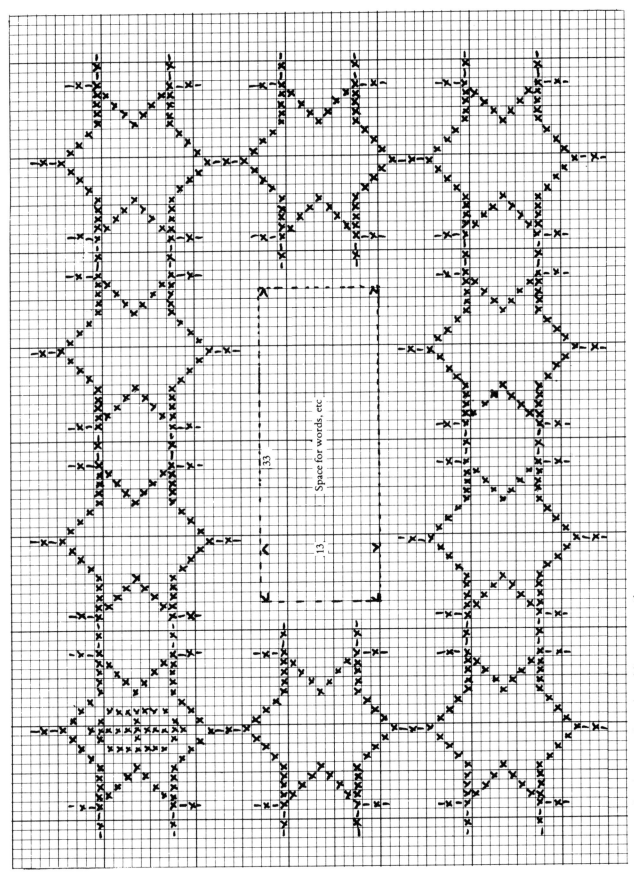

Space for words, etc

33

13

Fig 39 Star border 1 – enlarge by adding one motif

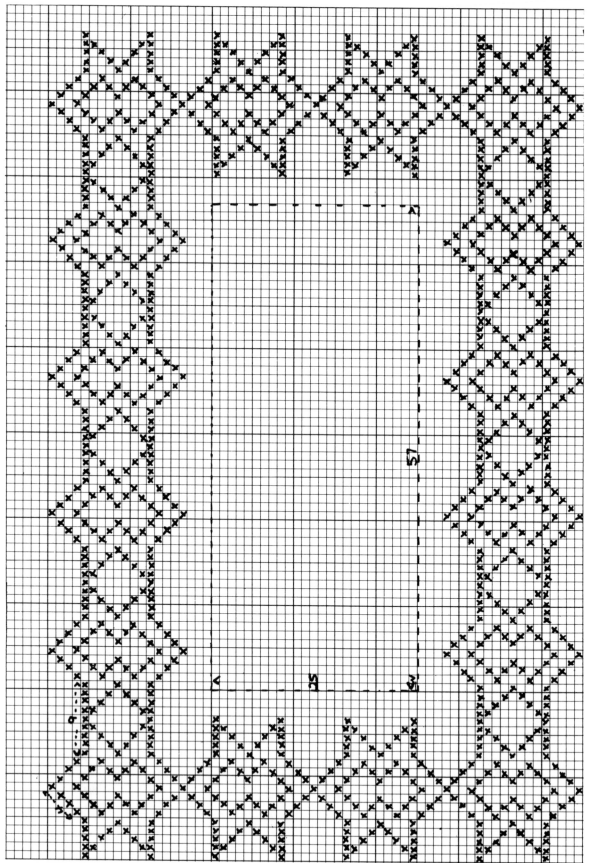

Fig 40 Star border 2 – enlarge or reduce by adding or leaving out one or more stars

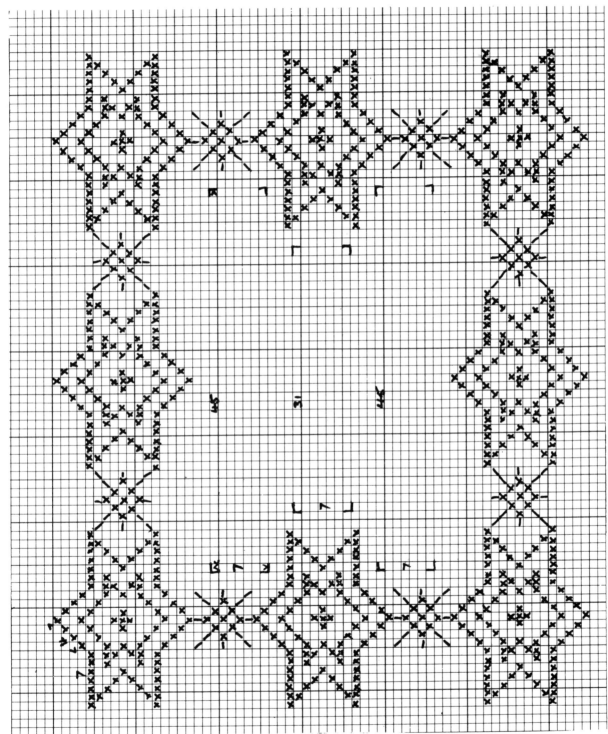

Fig 41 Star border 3 – enlarge by adding one small and one large star

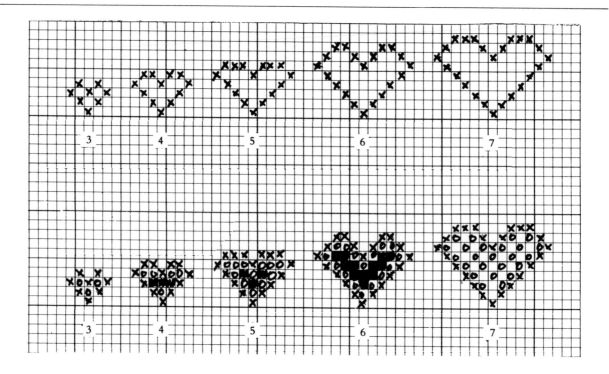

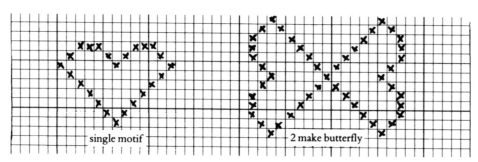

Fig 42 Hearts, showing various fillings and linked motifs to make butterflies and flowers

Again with the hearts I have graduated the size, and there are empty and filled hearts (Fig 42). How you place the hearts together will create new patterns – two will give a butterfly; three will turn a corner; four will make a flower. They can be linked in a variety of ways – with ends touching; with tops touching; with sides touching (Fig 43).

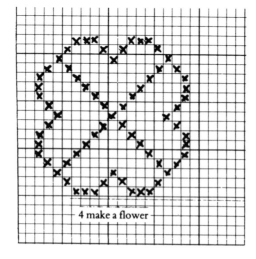

Maryann Kemp's sampler dated 1816, in the author's collection, contains many delightful contemporary motifs, while 'Remember Me' could become a charming heirloom to pass down through the family (see Figs 27 and 107 for charts)

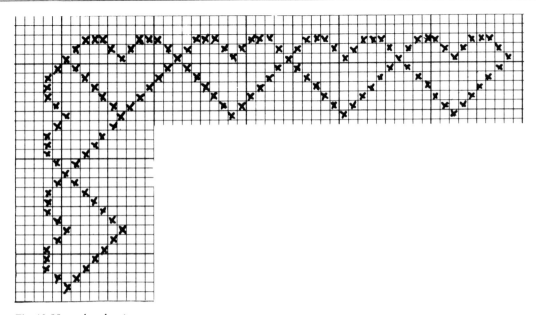

Fig 43 Heart border 1

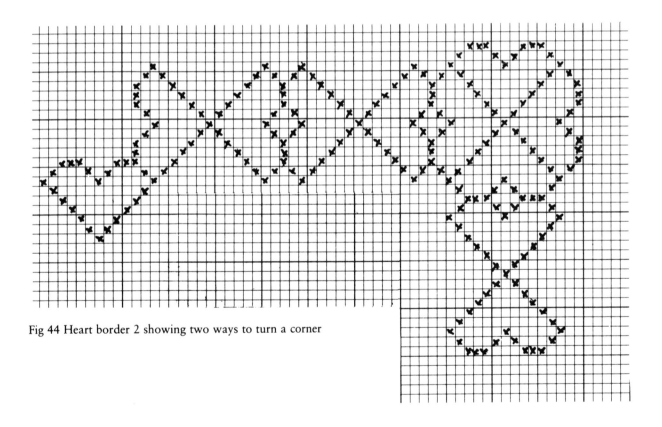

Fig 44 Heart border 2 showing two ways to turn a corner

Crosswords and commemorative designs make unusual
and lasting gifts (see Figs 22, 65, 71 and 76 for charts)

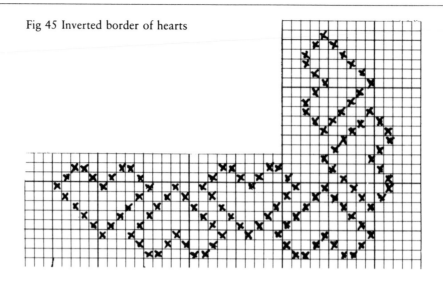

Fig 45 Inverted border of hearts

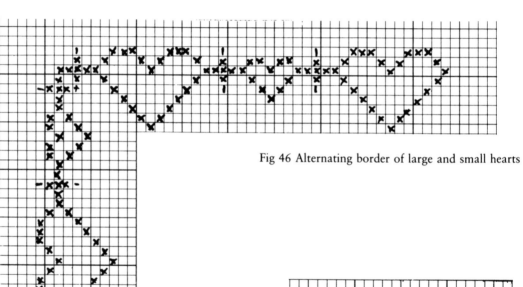

Fig 46 Alternating border of large and small hearts

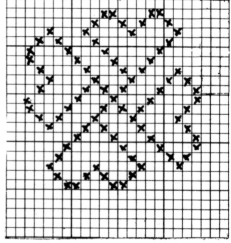

Fig 47 Rotating hearts

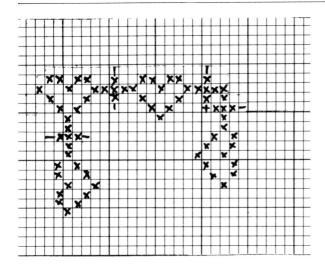

Fig 48 Border of small hearts showing two ways to turn a corner

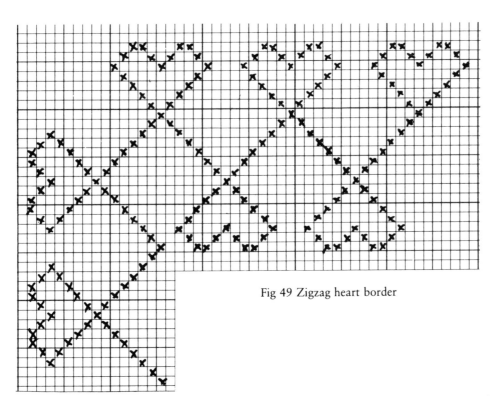

Fig 49 Zigzag heart border

Fig 44 gives two possible ways of turning a corner. Try inverting them or adding a cross to link them (Fig 45); vary the size of the heart (Fig 46); try to rotate them (Fig 47). Fig 48 shows two ways to turn a corner with a border of small hearts. Hearts can be used in a zigzag pattern (Fig 49), or the curve of the heart can be taken away to give a lattice effect (Fig 50).

Fig 51 is an example of a complete Greek Key border developing the sample shown earlier in the chapter. Experiment with other shapes – diamonds, triangles, circles, etc.

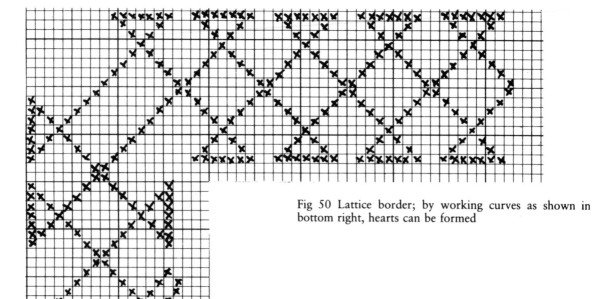

Fig 50 Lattice border; by working curves as shown in bottom right, hearts can be formed

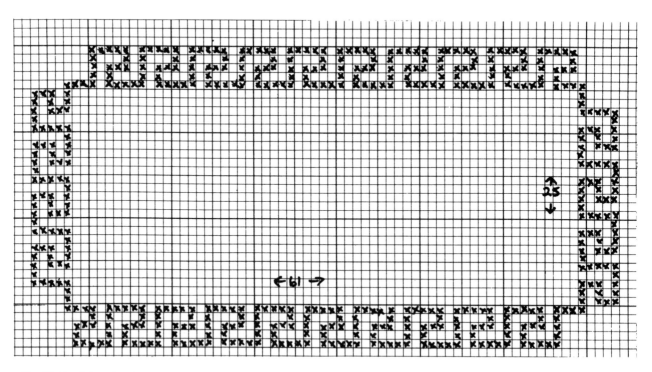

Fig 51 Greek key border

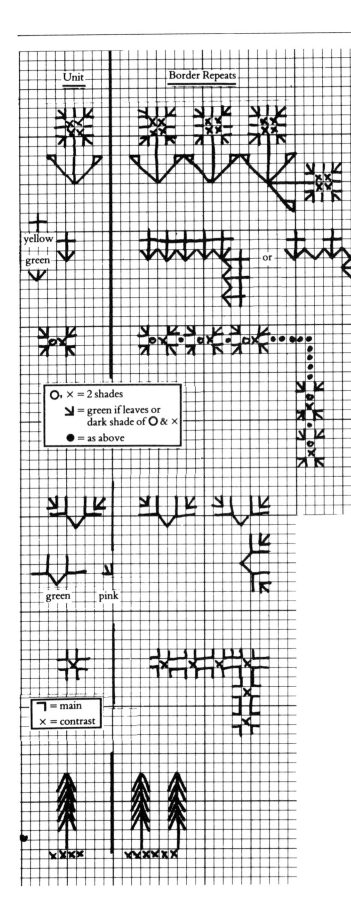

Small borders with flowers

Again using the basic unit idea, take a simple flower design and repeat it. Then decide upon a colour sequence to give variety. Develop it further by alternating the design with another flower pattern. Invert a second line to create a large and apparently complicated border. Figs 52–55 give a variety of ideas from my design notebooks.

Fig 52 Flower units developed into borders

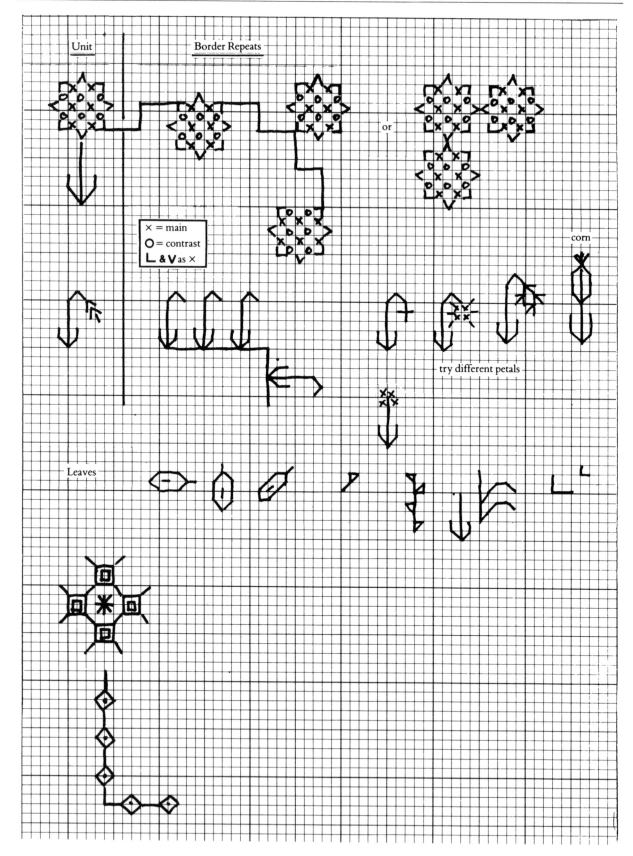

Fig 53 Flower and leaf units developed into borders

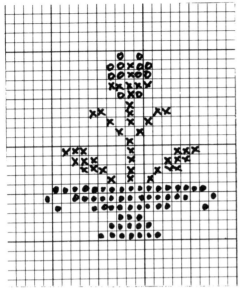

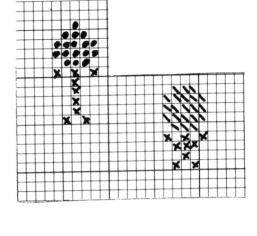

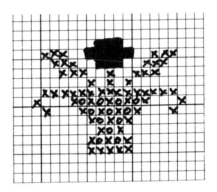

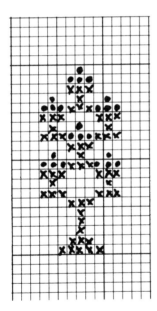

Fig 54 Motifs from the Maryann Kemp sampler

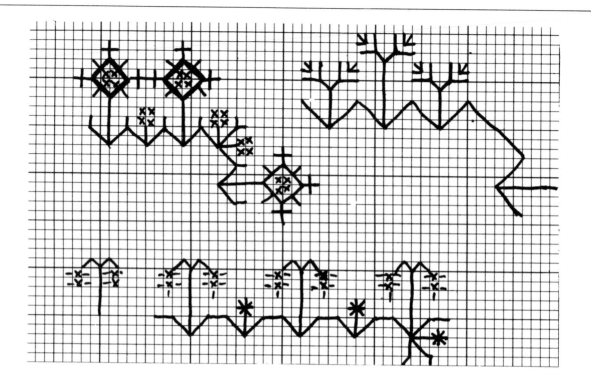

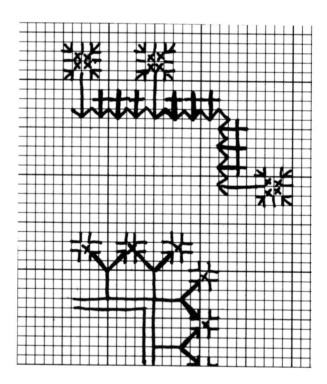

Fig 55 Combinations giving sequential patterns

The lavender motif

This motif will be found in various parts of the book. I have included it here as it demonstrates clearly how a single unit can be used in a variety of ways:

1 Individually (Fig 56) – see also Chapter 6.

2 Repeated as a linked border (Fig 57) – see 'Lavender's Blue' picture in Chapter 7.

3 As a single unit with a 1 up 1 down line of crosses, and a single line to divide each cross (Fig 58).

4 Four repeats used in a square to suggest spring, summer, autumn and winter by using different colours for the flowers – yellow for spring, lavender for summer, red/orange for autumn and white for winter (Fig 59).

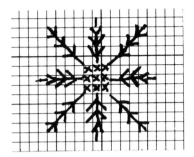

Fig 56

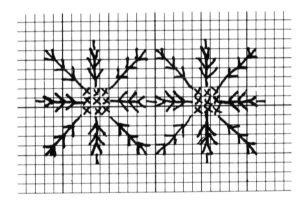

Fig 57

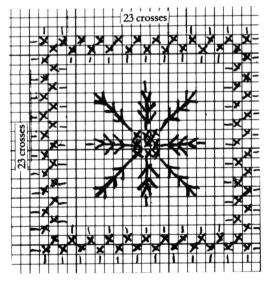

Fig 58

Fig 59

Small figures

Small figures such as animals, birds and people, can also be devised; there is plenty of scope for imagination here – and amusement too (Figs 60–62).

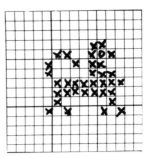

Fig 60

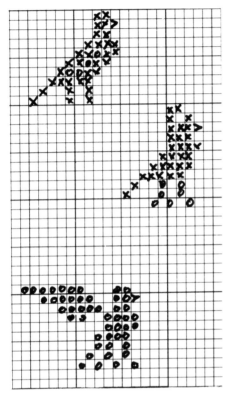

Fig 61

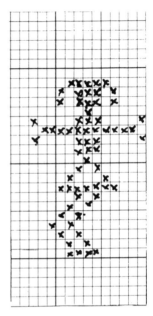

Fig 62

4
Crosswords and Commemorative Work

To work out a linked group of words or names you will need paper, graph paper, a pencil and a rubber. Lots of people like to have personalised things and this idea will help you to produce something special for the whole family. First write down the names of the people to be included. Take the longest and write it out in capitals. Then try to fit the other names to it finding common letters to link them together. Try different permutations until you are satisfied with the layout.

```
      D                    P
      A                    DANIEL
      N                        T   Y
PATRICK                  PETER     N
      E    E                  I
      T    LYN                C
      E                       K
      R
```

The first example is more compact and made the pictorial element of the house (the family unit) feasible (Fig 63). Fig 64 links the names Christine, Christopher, Roland and Katharine, while Fig 65 features Harriet, Timothy and Katherine, the children of Mary and Peter. Once you have decided upon the layout, plot the letters on graph paper. Next you must decide on the pictorial element. Think about the people in the crossword. What shared interests do they have? Perhaps they have pets, go sailing, are active in conservation; this will influence what you use for your decoration. You may decide to give it a pretty floral design with garlands and ribbons.

Sometimes it simply will not work if you only have two or three names as there may not be enough common letters. At other times it is possible to include the surname as well, as in the Grace family crossword (Fig 66).

Remember to use an alphabet that has all its letters the same height and width. Capitals are best for this kind of design.

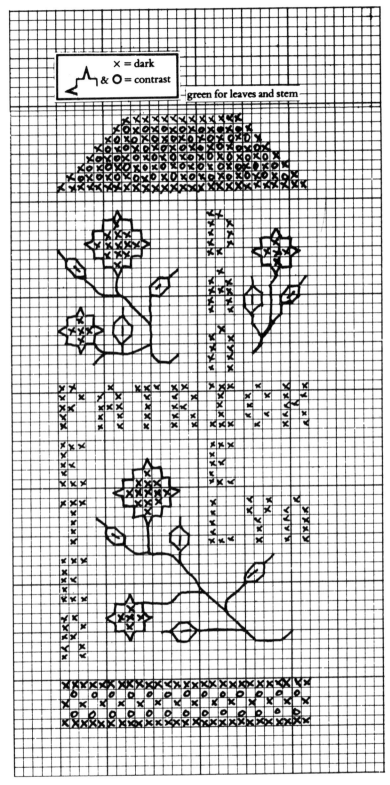

Fig 63

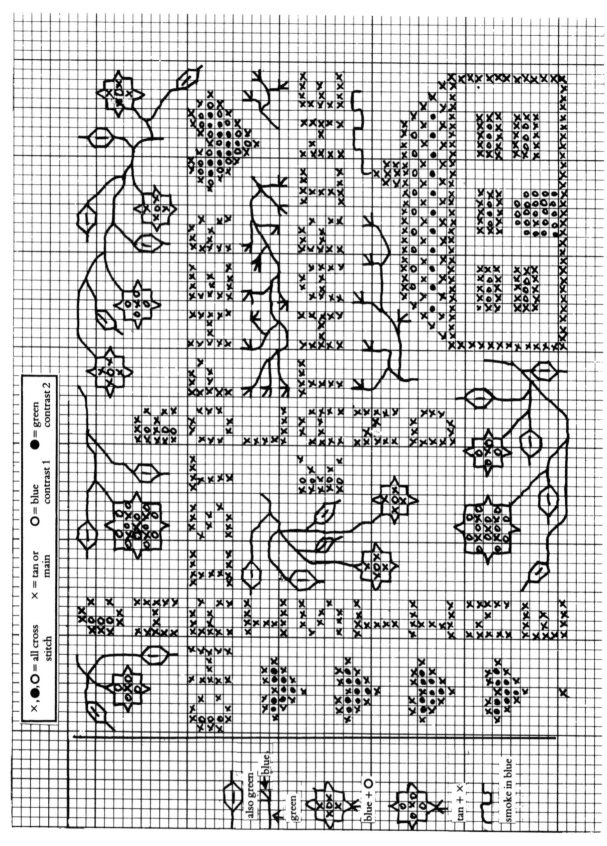

x, ●, O = all cross stitch

x = tan or main   O = blue contrast 1   ● = green contrast 2

also green

blue

green

blue + O

tan + x

smoke in blue

Fig 64

Fig 65

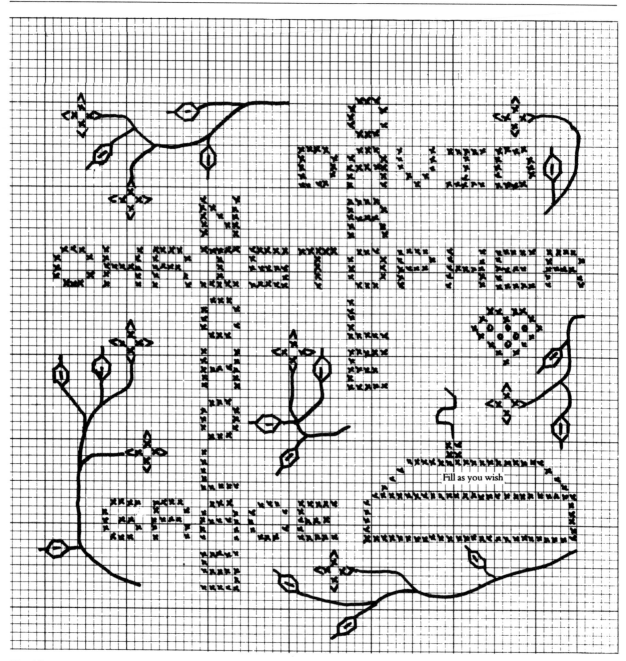

Fig 66

Designs for the seasons (see Figs 77, 78, 79, 80 and 84 for charts)

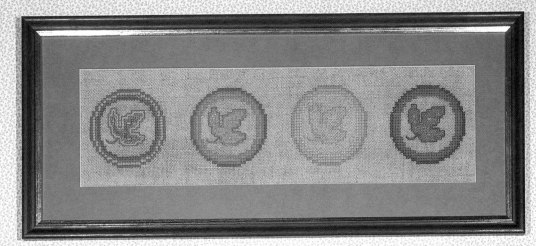

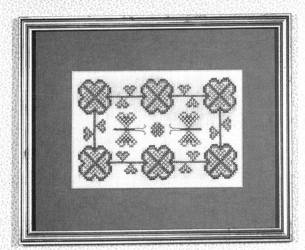

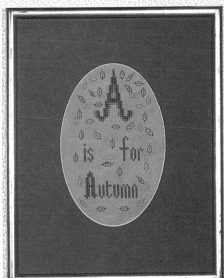

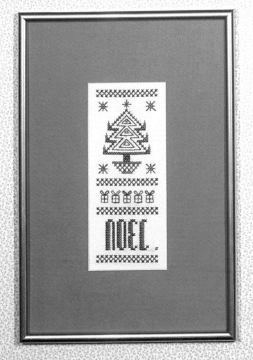

Commemorative work

Commemorative designs are really a specialised extension of Chapter 2, combined with the sections on borders and motifs in Chapter 3. What is the occasion? This is the time when you can make a more specialised use of colour.

Weddings

A sampler to commemorate a wedding is a lovely gift. Put in the couple's initials, the date and all the symbols of good luck for the future – bells, a knot, ribbons, a horseshoe, hearts. The project need not be a large one as you can see from the examples in Figs 67 and 68.

Silver, Ruby and Golden wedding anniversaries give further scope for designing (Figs 69, 70 and 71).

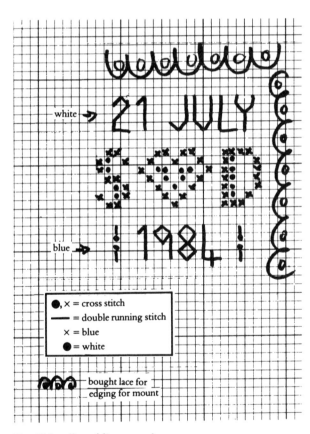

Fig 67 Small wedding sampler

Fig 68 Wedding sampler

An intriguing maze to commemorate St Valentine's Day and a celebration of the centenary of *The Mikado* (see Figs 89 and 117 for charts)

Fig 69 Silver wedding sampler

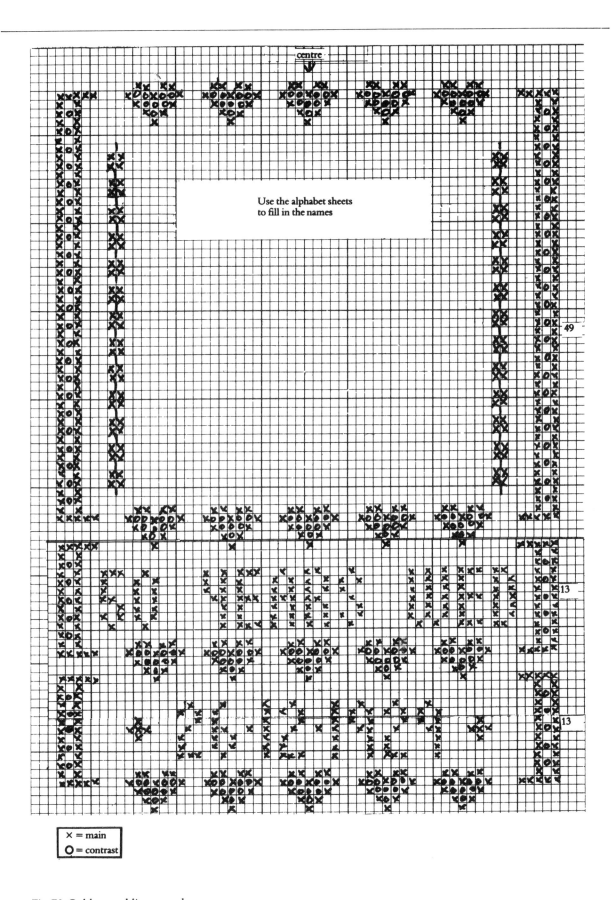

centre

Use the alphabet sheets
to fill in the names

49

13

13

× = main
O = contrast

Fig 70 Golden wedding sampler

Fig 71 Golden wedding sampler

Fig 72 Birth sampler

X = 3 x 3 holes incl
X = dark
V = dark
O = contrast
(if name is more than 6
letters, omit the diamonds)

Fig 73 Birth sampler

Birth samplers

Here I do feel you have to be careful with your
designs. Babies grow up very fast so I try to
stitch pictures that will appeal throughout the
child's life. The date, name and weight can be
included but personally I prefer just the name
and date with an attractive border around it
(Figs 72 and 73).

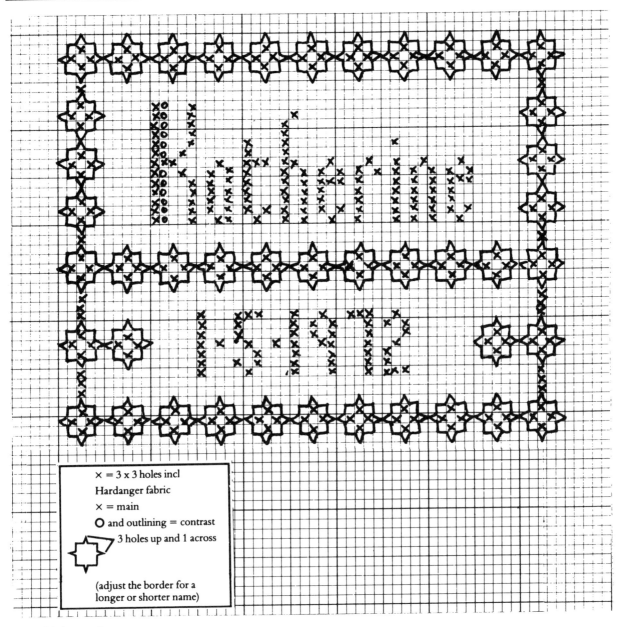

Fig 74 Birth sampler

Other events

Samplers for birthdays, particularly 18th or 21st birthdays, can be done in the same way (Fig 74). I have also stitched some for 40th birthdays.

Royal events and national occasions lend themselves to designing in a disciplined way. There are examples for the wedding of the Prince and Princess of Wales (Fig 75) and the centenary of one of the Gilbert & Sullivan operas (Fig 116 in Chapter 9). A suitable sampler can be worked as an unusual retirement gift (Fig 76).

If your work has a time limit, then you must plan out how you are going to stitch it. Be strict with yourself and do half an hour each day and stick to it. You must also allow time if you are having it framed.

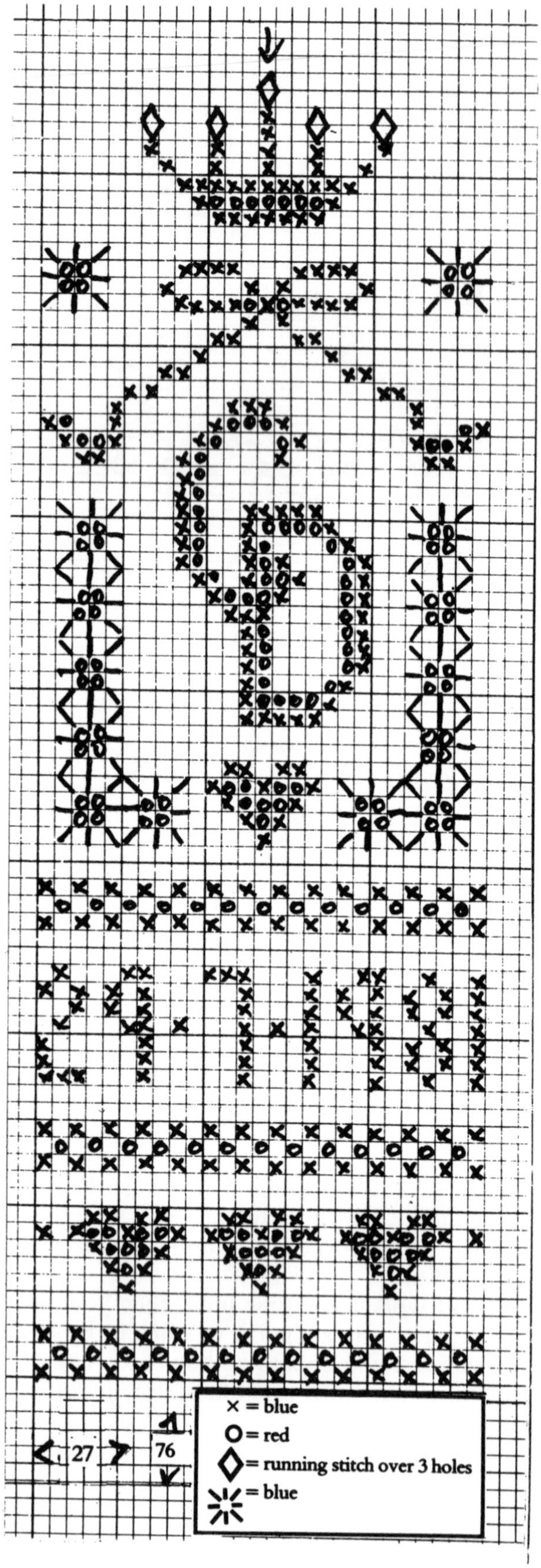

Fig 75 Royal Wedding sampler

Legend (within chart):
- × = blue
- O = red
- ◇ = running stitch over 3 holes
- ⚹ = blue

27   76

(*Opposite*) A wealth of ideas for simple projects, ideal for greetings cards, small gifts, bazaars and Christmas (see Figs 90, 91, 92, 98, 101, 102 and 103 for charts)

(*Page 82*) Large projects, though time-consuming, are very satisfying and give lasting pleasure (see Figs 105 and 106 for charts)

(*Page 83*) The author's personal sampler, worked to mark her fortieth birthday (see Fig 104 fo chart)

Fig 76 Retirement gift

Crossing the boundaries into other crafts; here the same
charted design is worked in cross stitch, filet crochet and
machine knitting (see Fig 108)

5
Designs for the Seasons

Designing for the seasons is rather like keeping a pictorial diary. As each year passes I find I am increasingly aware of the change of colour seen in nature and tend to think about each season as it approaches. I can't get inspired about Christmas in July! I suppose having taught young children for many years my working life has been geared to the turn of the seasons. The progression of the year with its ongoing continuity acts as a framework for life. In the past feasts and festivals represented anchors for people whose lives were so tied up with religious events.

Inspiration can come from anywhere and usually when you least expect it – a chance remark, a quote from a poem, a carving on a park bench, even grafitti. Keep your notebook handy as your memory is not always accurate.

The designs I have included were worked over a period of five years – different seasons in different years. Time, of which there is never enough, limits the output of work. I find I do most of my designs in the holidays when I am free from outside pressures and stitch them at my leisure during term time.

A is for Autumn (Fig 77)

Fabric – fine Glenshee in gold.
Stranded cotton in autumn shades.
The design was built around a complex letter A stitched in three tones. The letters are spaced to balance the A and a simple capital is used for autumn. I have only plotted a few leaves so you can judge for yourself where to put the others. Draw them in before you stitch.

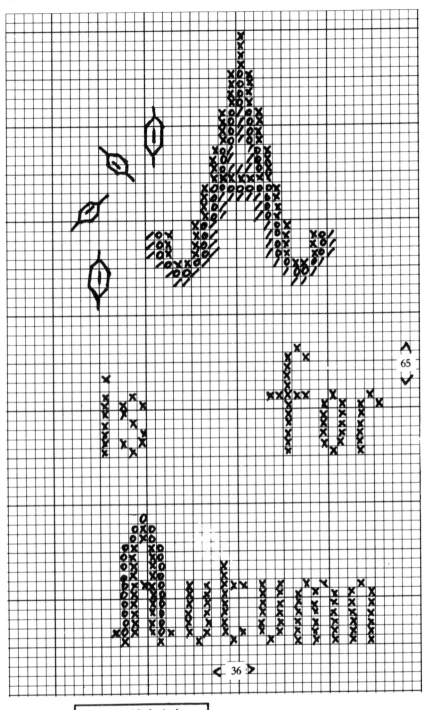

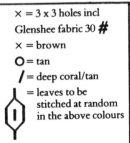

x = 3 x 3 holes incl
Glenshee fabric 30 **#**

x = brown

O = tan

/ = deep coral/tan

= leaves to be
stitched at random
in the above colours

Fig 77 Autumn sampler

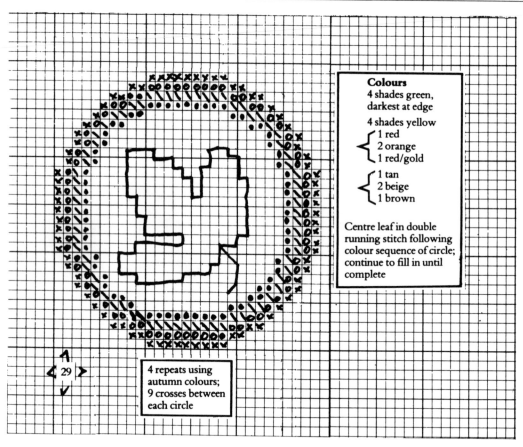

Colours

4 shades green, darkest at edge

4 shades yellow

{ 1 red
2 orange
1 red/gold

{ 1 tan
2 beige
1 brown

Centre leaf in double running stitch following colour sequence of circle; continue to fill in until complete

4 repeats using autumn colours; 9 crosses between each circle

29

Fig 78 Seasonal sampler

Autumn/Fall Circles (Fig 78)

Ecru linen
2 strands each of stranded cotton in:
3 tones of green
3 tones of yellow
3 tones of red/orange
3 tones of brown

I spent one autumn term with my Adult Education Class exploring circles. These were used as a frame outline with a motif stitched inside. Here is my design. The circles symbolize the sun and the fullness of the harvest time encircling the leaves in their changing colour tone. The circle also gives the continuity of the seasons turning full circle. You cannot achieve a true curve as the nature of cross stitch necessitates a series of steps, but you can get a good result.

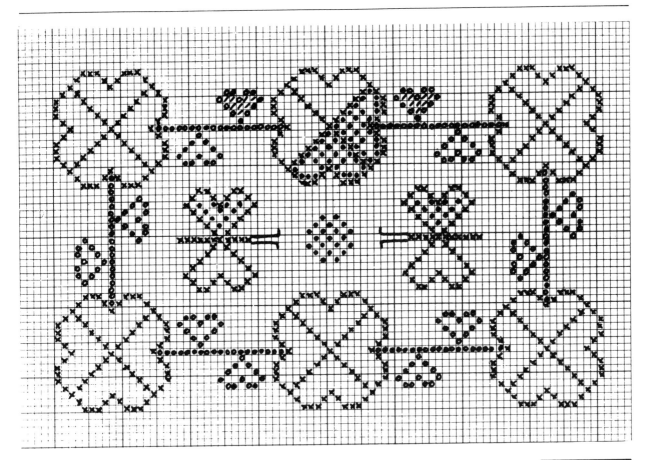

Fig 79 Summer sampler; complete the shapes using the examples given

Summer (Fig 79)

Fine linen
2 strands of stranded cotton in 2 blues and 2 greens

This design is purely pictorial. It uses the heart motif singly as leaves, with two for a butterfly and four for the pansy flowerhead. It is reminiscent of a formal Elizabethan garden. It is important to centre this design.

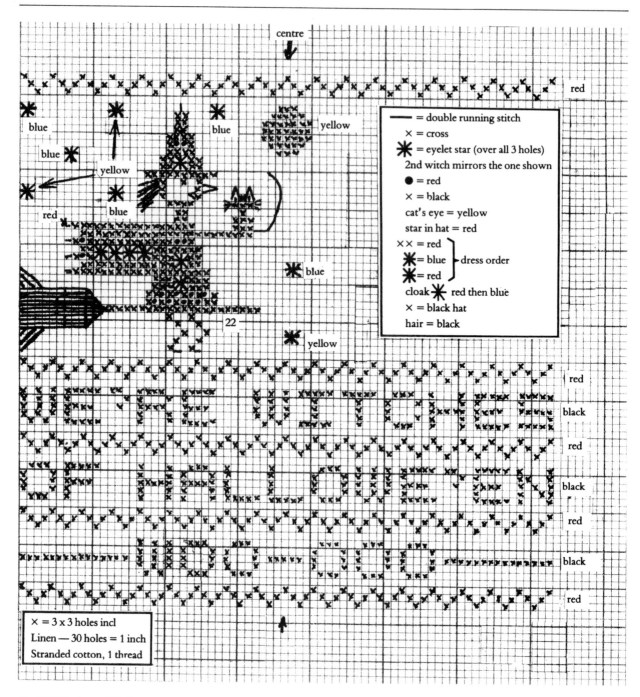

Fig 80 Witches of Hallowe'en

We're Witches of Hallowe'en (Fig 80)

Fine linen
1 thread of stranded cotton or silk (black)

This was a very mathematical design using basic shapes such as triangle, square and zigzag. The two witches are mirror images of each other and the background is strictly balanced. The zigzag borders give continuity to the design.

Noel

Hardanger fabric
2 strands of red and green stranded cotton

I think it is important to preserve the traditions of the past but to remember to make our own contribution. Christmas specials are nice to have to bring out each year. Noel has been worked in two ways to show the variation of the motif and the reversal of colour. It began with the small unit of one word (Fig 81). Fig 82 shows repeats grouped as a star, while Fig 83 shows the units grouped as a garland or holly wreath. Fig 84 shows other Christmas motifs arranged in a less formal design. There are other small Christmas ideas in Chapter 6.

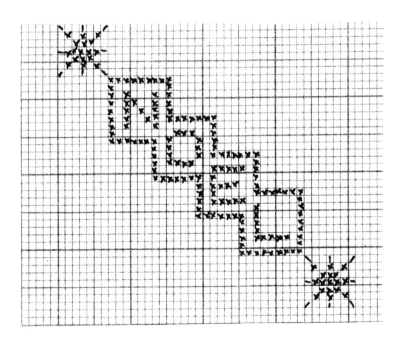

Fig 81 Simple Noel design

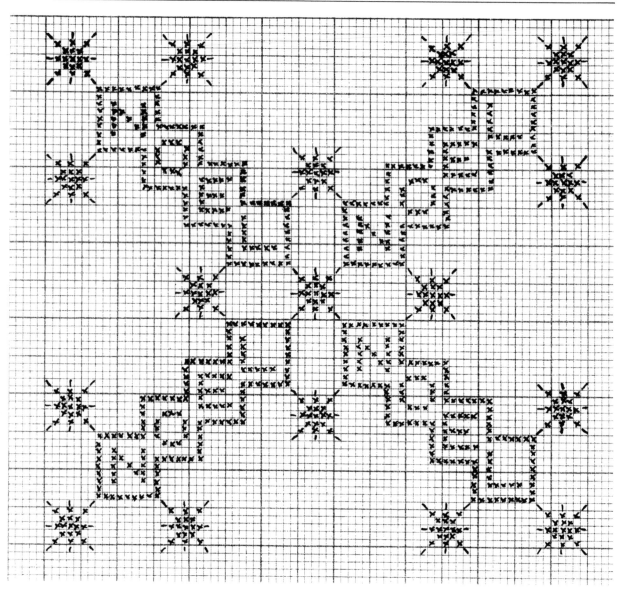

Fig 82 Repeated Noel design to form star

Cross stitch interpretations of a series of traditional patchwork designs together with, in the centre, a design based on a carpet pattern (see Figs 110–116 for charts)

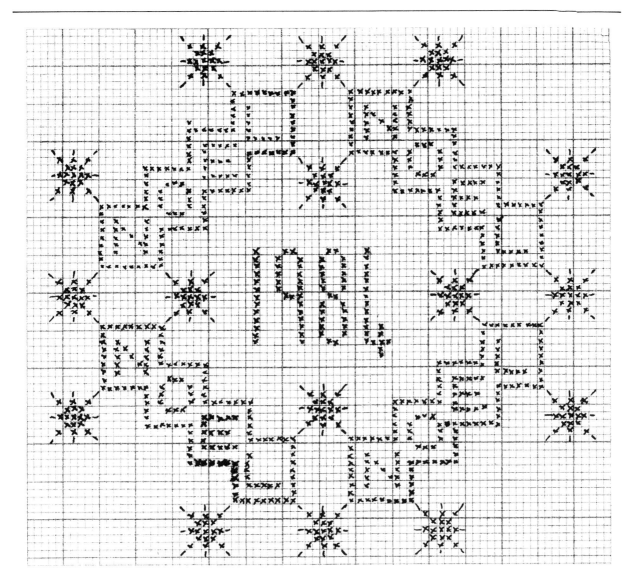

Fig 83 Repeated Noel design to form garland

Two designs with a floral theme: (*above*) inspired by
Elizabethan knot gardens, (*below*) to commemorate 1985
as The Year of the Garden (see Figs 118 and 127 for charts)

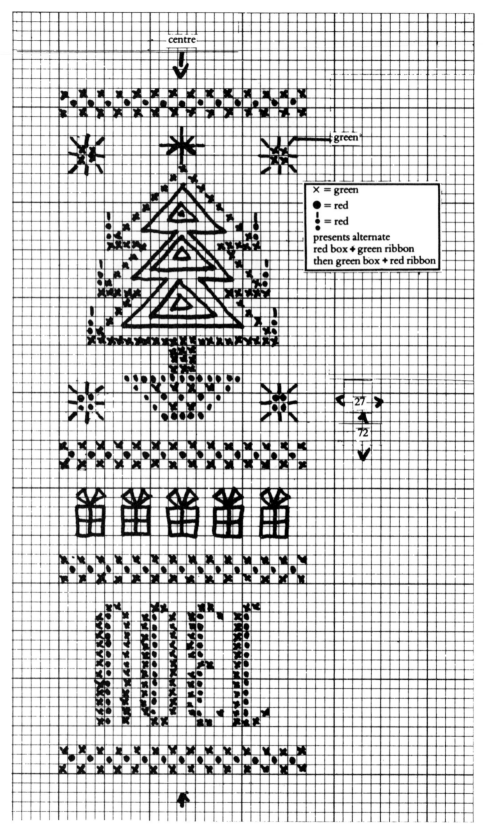

Fig 84 Christmas motifs

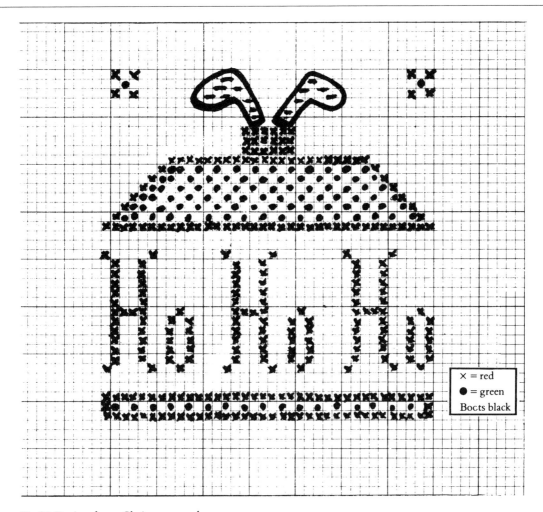

Fig 85 Design for a Christmas card

Ho Ho Ho (Fig 85)

A small design to be put in a card or small frame, just a bit of fun. Humour is very important as it preserves our sanity and stops us getting too pompous.

Valentine's Day projects

The obvious motif is the heart and I have included four variations. Fig 86 shows a small B inside the heart, quick to do especially if you have forgotten the date! It can be mounted for a card – see Chapter 6. In Fig 87 the heart border leaves a centre large enough for an initial. I worked the border first and then the letter. Fig 88 shows an enlarged treatment of Fig 87, giving enough space for about seven letters.

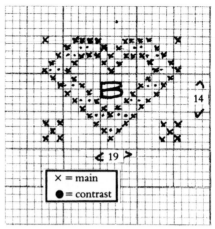

Fig 86 Simple heart motif

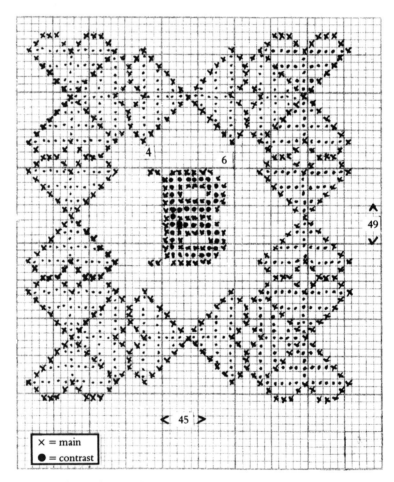

Fig 87 A design for a Valentine

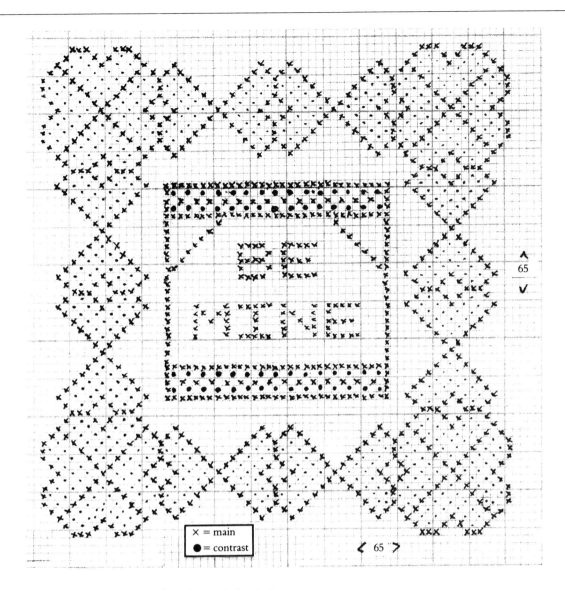

Fig 88 A heart border giving room for a longer Valentine's Day message

Fig 89 'The way to my heart' was great fun to design and stitch, but I had to keep my wits about me while doing it. I worked it on fine cotton fabric with black silk thread and a little red stranded cotton. It also needed a good working light to prevent mistakes. There are three false ways and one true. Plot the true one first, then you will see what you have left to fill.

Begin at the centre with the heart and work to the points of entry.

Have a look in books or in museums for labyrinth patterns. Visit Roman villas where there is a wealth of designs to be found or go to Hampton Court Maze. It is stimulating to take a design from the past and give it a new interpretation.

Linen 32 #
Stranded cotton, 1 strand
× = black
O & ─ ─ = red

Fig 89 A fascinating and most unusual Valentine

6
Small Gifts

This chapter provides a variety of small projects which will give a quick and pleasing result. They are suitable for gifts for special people, sales of work and school bazaars.

A birthday card

You can stitch a small design on fabric using the ideas shown in Fig 90. Or why not try out a Victorian idea – that of using perforated paper. Normal cross stitch techniques are used but care must be taken not to pull the thread too hard or the paper will tear. Use strands of stranded cotton and a suitable tapestry needle. Use the paper on the smooth side and do not put it in a ring or roller frame. Try slide binders if you are working a large piece to keep the tension right. A selection of designs for perforated paper is given in Fig 92.

A calendar

Using the chart provided (Fig 91), stitch the picture or design your own. Trim and press the work lightly and stick it on to a bought calendar mount. The one shown is a photographic mount.

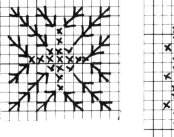
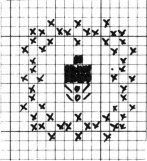
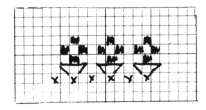

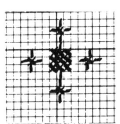

Fig 90 A variety of simple designs for greetings cards

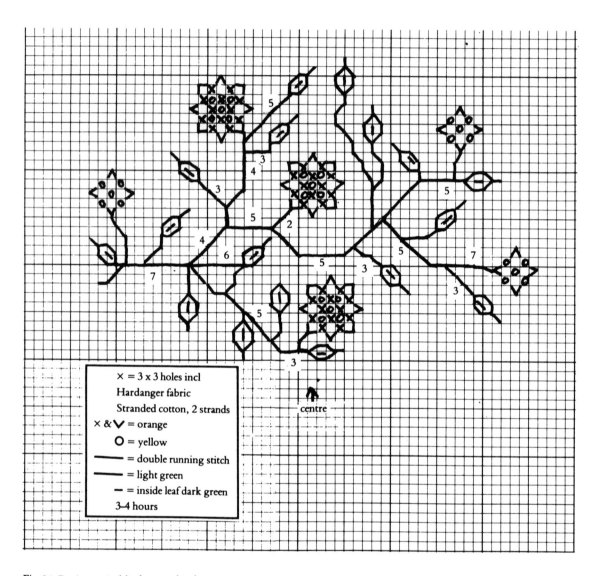

Fig 91 Design suitable for a calendar

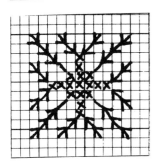

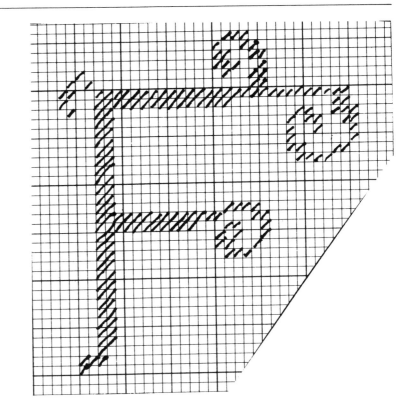

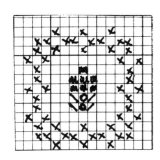

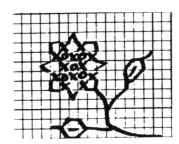

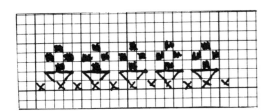

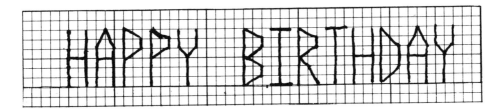

Fig 92 Designs suitable for working on perforated paper;
HAPPY BIRTHDAY is worked in double running stitch

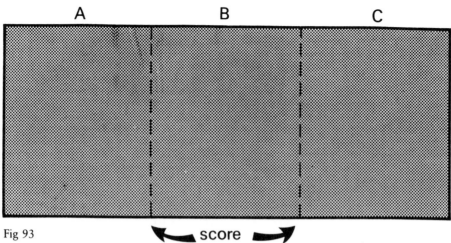

Fig 93

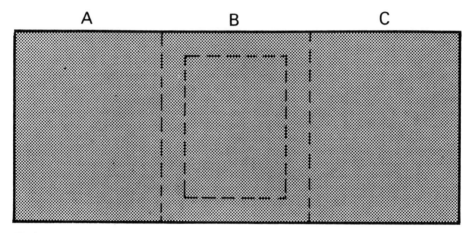

Fig 94

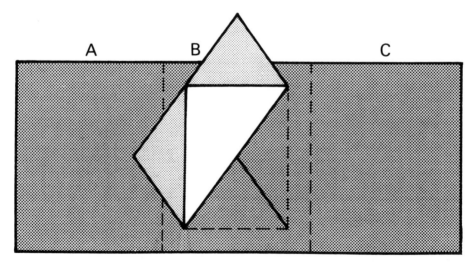

Fig 95

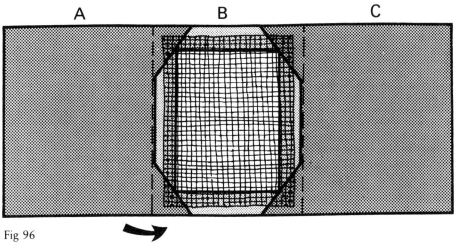

A   B   C

Fig 96

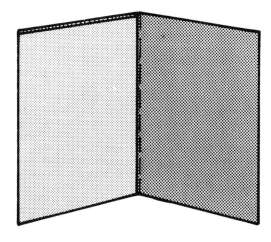

To mount your work

1 Cut a piece of thin card allowing half as much length again as the finished size of the card. This will be folded back to cover the back of your work (Fig 93).

2 Divide into three sections and score with scissors or a knife to make a neat fold.

3 On the middle section B mark a window the required size allowing for a small border round your design. Score again (Fig 94).

4 Cut diagonally to each corner and fold back. Trim away any paper that shows above the top and bottom of the card (Fig 95).

5 Glue down the cut pieces of the window and hold firmly to get a sharp fold.

6 Place your design right side down on the opening and glue in place (Fig 96).

7 Glue A all over and stick to B (Fig 96).

8 The inside is now ready for your message (Fig 97).

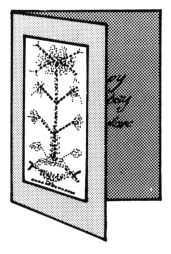

Fig 97

Bought frames

You can get some delightful small frames either for pictures or for lids of pots or boxes. They are quick to make and look very professional when finished. Wooden frames are also available.

Star design (Fig 98)

Check your design will fit into the frame without being crowded. If not, you may need to work on finer fabric. The one I used has an acetate sheet, a metal ring and a backing card.

When your work is ready:

1 Press your work on the back with a steam iron.
2 Centre and glue it to the backing card.
3 Trim away the excess material.
4 Cover with the acetate sheet and press it into the ring. Check that it is in the centre, in line with the hanger. Also be careful you have not trapped any loose threads, hair or dust on the acetate sheet.
5 Make a twist or plait to hang it by. Cut the threads twice as long as the required finished length. Tie to a fixed point and knot the other end. Hold between your thumb and index finger and insert a pencil between the threads. Turn the pencil round and round until the threads are tightly twisted (Fig 99). Fold in half, let go the folded end and the twist will even out (Fig 100). Cut and tie the end off neatly.

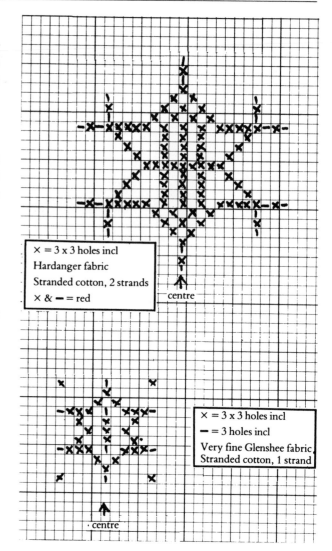

× = 3 x 3 holes incl
Hardanger fabric
Stranded cotton, 2 strands
× & — = red

× = 3 x 3 holes incl
— = 3 holes incl
Very fine Glenshee fabric
Stranded cotton, 1 strand

centre

Fig 98 Star designs for a round frame and a box lid

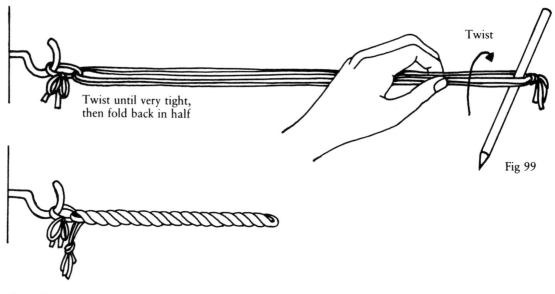

Twist

Twist until very tight, then fold back in half

Fig 99

Fig 100

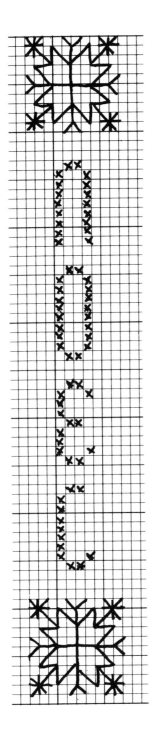

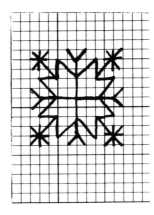

Fig 101 Motifs for Christmas napkins and table centre

Box lid

This is a smaller version of the above. Nice for an initial or a single flower and very quick. Mount in the same way.

Buttons

Working your own tiny designs for buttons will personalise a jacket or blouse quickly and easily.

Do not use too thick a fabric or it may be hard to do up the button. Some woollen fabrics are evenweave and can be stitched in this way.

Christmas napkins (Fig 101)

Make a set of napkins for your Christmas table or as a present. You need 1⅔yd (1½m) of Aida fabric to give you 6 large napkins. This fabric is very easy to use and no frame is needed. Cut into 18in (45cm) squares, very carefully following the line of the weave.

Stitch a motif in the corner of each napkin, finishing off very neatly. Fringe the edges. It is not necessary to stitch the edges as the fabric is very firm. Press lightly. The napkins will wash well.

Table centre (Fig 101)

Use an off-cut of Aida fabric and stitch Noël and some stars to go with the napkins.

Lavender bags (Fig 102)

The motif is a star variation and the colours were inspired by the lavender fields at Heacham, Norfolk. You will need 2 pieces of fabric 5in (12.5cm) square.

1 Stitch the design on one piece.
2 Press.
3 Put right sides together; pin and stitch using double running stitch, carefully matching the two pieces together hole for hole.
4 Leave a hole, turn the bag. Press and fill with lavender.
5 Catch stitch the hole. Make a plait (see Figs 99 & 100) and stitch in place. Then tie a bow.

Fig 103 gives an alternative design for a small bag for herbs or to keep jewellery in.

Cushion variation

By working four lavender motifs (Fig 102) together in a square, you could stitch a larger design and sew it into a cushion, simply appliquéing it into position.

An initial paperweight

You will need a glass paperweight, 2 card discs, 1 self-adhesive velour backing circle, fabric and thread.

Stitch a design that will fit into the paperweight. Some will magnify the pattern. Press with a steam iron on the back.

To assemble the paperweight:
1 Glue around the edge of one of the card discs, then push the material firmly down. Use a clear adhesive.

2 Trim to ¼in (5mm) around the disc, fold back and glue in place. Let the glue nearly dry before pushing down.
3 Glue the second disc to the first to cover the raw edges of the material.
4 Push the initial into the paperweight – it should be a tight fit – and cover with the velour disc. Trim to neaten.

Remember to remove fingermarks from the glass before assembling.

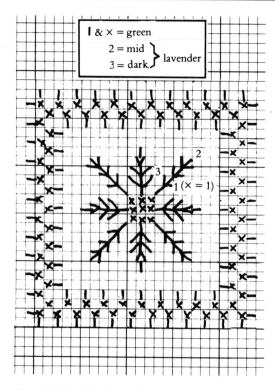

Fig 102 Motif for lavender bag

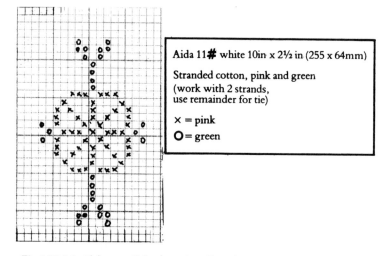

Fig 103 Motif for small herb or jewellery bag

7
Large Projects

Major projects demand a lot of thought even before you begin to put your ideas down on paper. Like a dog worrying a bone, once you start you can't leave it alone. When stitching a large piece, protect the fabric on the roller with tissue or polythene so that your hands do not rub on the work already completed.

My sampler to commemorate my fortieth birthday (Fig 104)

The aim of this piece was to give my own personal interpretation of a sampler. I did much research from books and made visits to museums; there are some lovely examples in the Fitzwilliam Museum in Cambridge and in the Victoria and Albert Museum in London.

I decided to use an alphabet from an old sampler that I own to keep some continuity with the past. The lay-out incorporated the alphabet in two rows with different line borders used as underlining all the way through; a line of numbers; a motto 'May all your dreams come true'; a large rectangle divided into sixteen boxes surrounding a smaller rectangle.

There are three outer borders from different periods – the eighteenth, nineteenth and twentieth centuries. The boxes are filled with my seven cats, each filled with a different stitch to keep the sampler element of passing on different techniques. The remaining boxes represent the things I enjoy doing: tap dancing, spinning, music, the countryside and conservation, sewing and keep fit. My husband's and my own birth signs are included and I signed it with a computer box to reflect 'now'. In the centre I stitched the year we got married with our initials and the tree of life. Accurate counting was absolutely essential. The borders were very complicated and did involve the odd cheat here and there.

The sampler was worked on hardanger fabric with stranded cottons, perlé, gold and silver threads and a bead; three strands were generally used, but occasionally six strands and single strands were used. In addition to cross stitch, other stitches used were double running stitch (Holbein), chain stitch, needle weaving over warp threads, Jacquard, Assisi, satin stitch, Florentine, tent stitch over warp threads, couching, bound stack (sheaves), running stitch with interwoven thread and with fine thread, blanket stitch, herringbone stitch, Gobelin and star stitch worked over warp threads (back over one and forward under two which forms a spiral when pulled tight).

The sampler took nearly six months to complete; I divided it up into weekly targets and kept pretty well to them. The working order was:

1 The alphabet
2 The numbers
3 The motto
4 The outline and filling of the boxes
5 The centre with date and initials
6 The inside border
7 The middle border
8 The outer border

Although there is a lot to think about with work of this size, do not be put off. There is a great deal of satisfaction to be enjoyed by tackling a major project.

March Winds and April Showers (Fig 105)

The first large piece of work I did was 'March winds and April showers'. I planned it in the same way as described in chapter 2.

The placing of the words came first. These were set in four lines with each alternate line placed above its fellow:

March	winds	and
	April	showers
Bring	forth	
	May	flowers

I wanted a fairly elaborate script but one where the capitals were not too complicated as these would vie with the pictorial element. Black stranded cotton was used for the letters but with each capital having a contrast colour suitable to the area of design.

The picture was built up bit by bit. The tree, worked in stem stitch and filled with crosses, was arched to give the feel of the force of the wind. April showers was easy to illustrate – a cloud outline in creams and greys, with running stitch for the rain highlighted with a few sequins. May flowers became a sample of all sorts of flower designs with clusters and trails; there is plenty of scope here for further inventiveness.

When doing a large piece it is essential to have enough fabric. I usually have far more than I need just in case I change my mind and want to add to the design. Do not feel you must always stick to your original pattern; look critically at your work as you go along and be ready to change if necessary.

This picture did not rely on a complicated border or a strict discipline – I was not ready for that when I stitched it in 1981. The balance of the design was governed strictly by eye.

Lavender's Blue (Fig 106)

This was inspired by the lavender fields in flower last year which I passed every day on my way to work. I designed the lavender motif already seen in Chapters 3 and 6 and the border grew from this.

It is a very strictly disciplined piece. Lavender is grown commercially in straight rows and there are many varieties which gave scope for tonal colour. There is a colour repeat in the work.

I used the familiar rhyme as it seemed so appropriate. The lettering was worked out with underlining in different colours. Hearts were used to fill out the lines, and the border has a linked design added to it. It took about six weeks to complete; once the lettering was set the rest followed easily. The border was a bit repetitive to do, so I worked three or four motifs a day and had other work in progress at the same time.

I used écru linen for the background and two strands of Danish Flower threads together which have a matt finish and soft colour. The piece measures 162×112 crosses.

Maryann Kemp sampler (Fig 107)

This sampler, which was worked in 1816, shows traditional lettering, a simple border and a multiplicity of interesting motifs reflecting the period. It was interesting to see from a look at the back just how much the original colours had faded.

A colourful interpretation of the four seasons (see Fig 119 for chart)

Border 1 (outer)
× = turquoise
°,° = tan
/ = grey

Border 2
● = green
× = turquoise

Border 3
°°° = tan
✓,✓ = grey

Letters & numbers
× = turquoise (A line)
× = green (border)
O line = tan
border = grey
/ = turquoise
outline green

Motto
× = tan ("May all your")
× = turquoise ("Dreams")
× = tan ("Come true")
× = blue (stars)
⌐Κ = blue and grey (stars)

Box
× = turquoise (outline)

Cat top left (1)
× = green outlined in turquoise

Cat (2)
× = grey
▲ = green & tan

Cat (3)
× = turquoise (centre)
blanket = grey
⊠ = grey & silver thread

Cat (4)
× = brown (tan)
    couched with green
herringbone = green

Cat (5)
Woven star
brown (tan) weaving
× = turquoise
sheaves = brown

Cat (6)
× = grey
steps alternate green & grey

Cat (7)
× = turquoise
grey warp threads
turquoise weaving
grey chain

Tap (8)
shoes = turquoise
taps = grey

Wheel (9)
wheel = tan
band = turquoise

Recorder (10)
green & brown

Flowers (11)
turquoise & green

Sewings (12)
outline = grey
sewing = turquoise

Scorpio (13)
turquoise & green

Keep fit (14)
tan & green

Capricorn (15)
turquoise

Computer signature (16)
green

Key to Fig 104 on next page

Narrow borders used to suggest hedges and mazes, and experiments with flower head designs (see Figs 121 and 123–126 for charts)

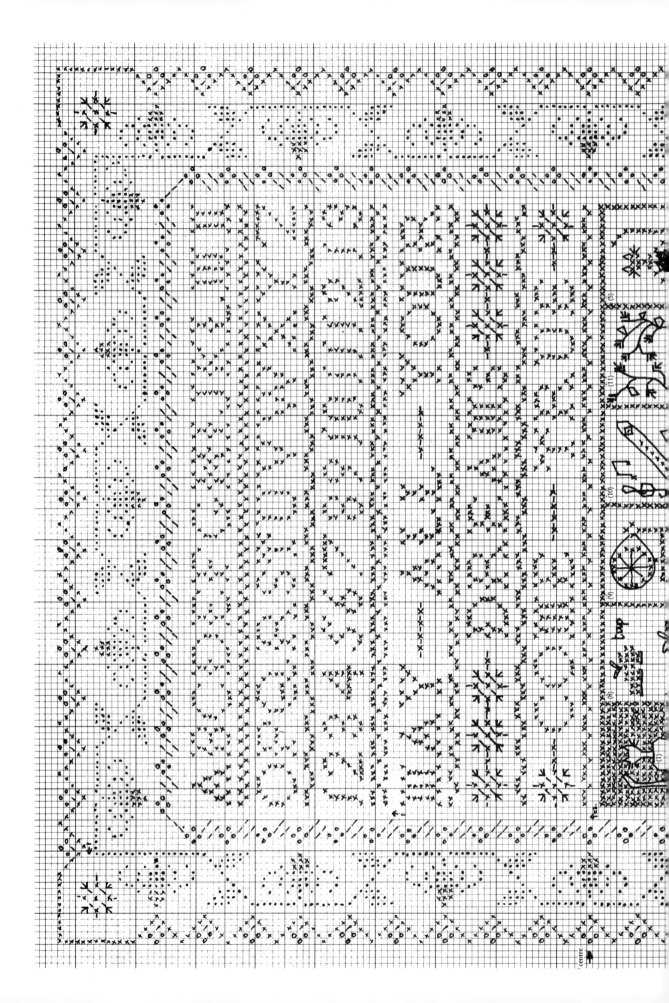

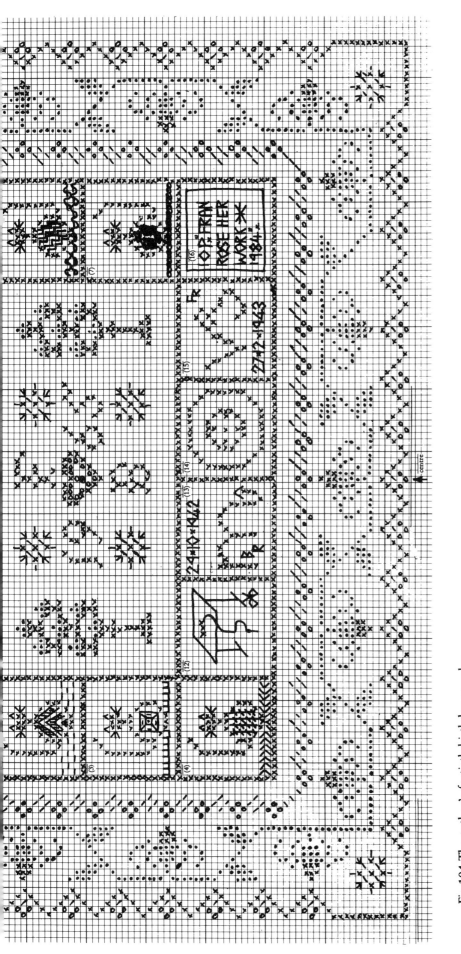

Fig 104 The author's fortieth birthday sampler

Branches

3 lines stem stitch over 3 holes in brown, tan and cream

Trunk

Stem stitch over 6 holes, brown outside, then tan, then cream

Crosses to fill as you please

× = brown

O = cream

March winds

April

Bring forth

May

Flower heads

× = dark pink

\ll/ = light pink

Stem & leaves mid green

mid blue

mid green

gold

mid green

light pink

dark pink

Flower

W = mid green

+ = gold

Flowers

O & × = 2 tones blue

leaves = dark green

dark green | purple

⌐ light blue

N lavender

light green stems

mid green | alternate blue & purple

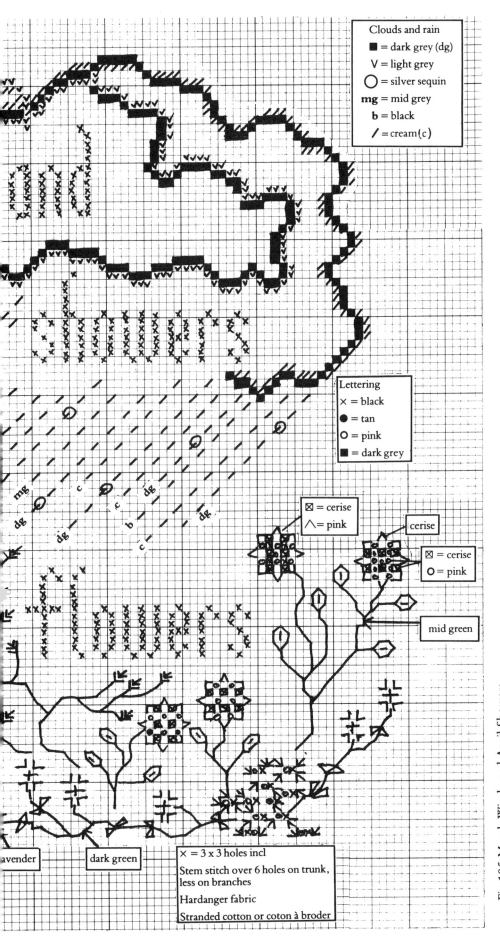

Clouds and rain
■ = dark grey (dg)
V = light grey
◯ = silver sequin
mg = mid grey
b = black
╱ = cream (c)

Lettering
× = black
● = tan
○ = pink
■ = dark grey

⊠ = cerise
∧ = pink

cerise

⊠ = cerise
○ = pink

mid green

lavender

dark green

× = 3 x 3 holes incl

Stem stitch over 6 holes on trunk,
less on branches

Hardanger fabric

Stranded cotton or coton à broder

Fig 105 March Winds and April Showers

Cheat here over 5 holes

① = purple
② = lavender/blue tone
③ = pinkish purple
④ = light green
⑤ = dark green
⑥ = light pinkish purple (tones with 3)

Cheat here
over 5 holes

Cheat here
over 5 holes

Cheat here
over 5 holes

Fig 106 Lavender's Blue

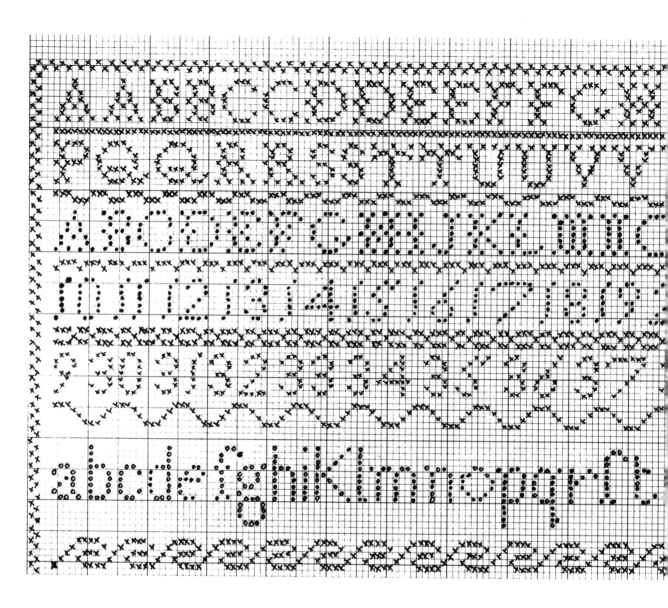

Fig 107 Maryann Kemp sampler (cont on following page)

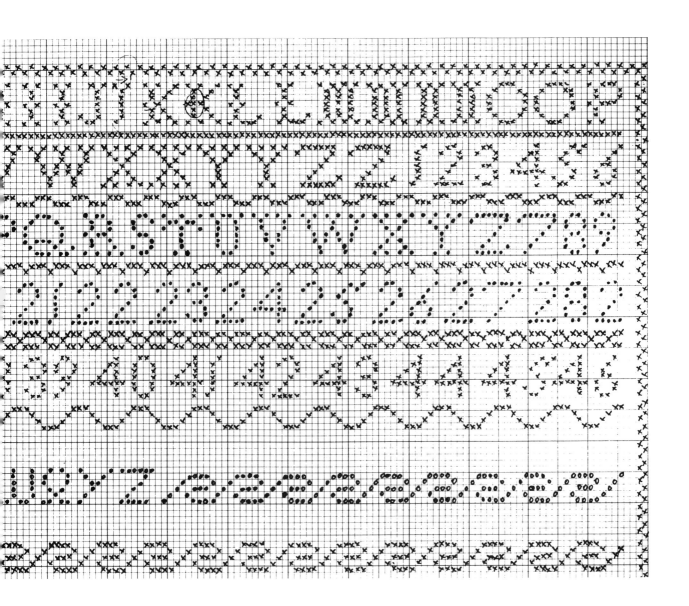

Fig 107 Maryann Kemp sampler (cont)

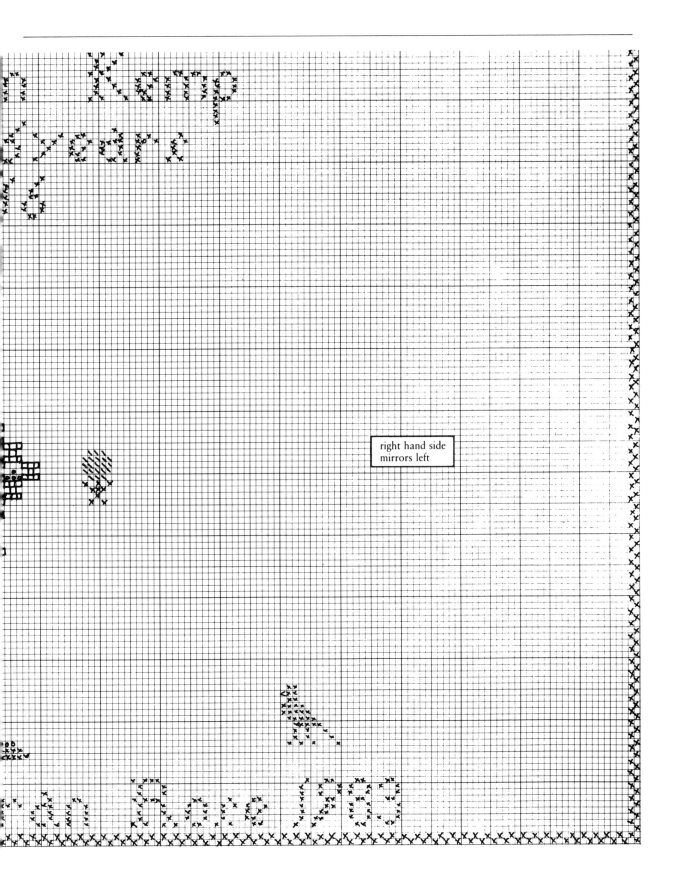

right hand side
mirrors left

8
Crossing the Boundaries

The preceding chapters have shown the techniques whereby you can confidently create your own cross stitch designs. You may now like to look beyond the restrictions of one craft and be ready to adapt and experiment in other fields – to look for the similarity in other crafts. For example, my friend Vanessa Bowron, a crochet tutor, came across an old pattern for filet crochet. It was a charted pattern for a table centre and a tea-cosy. She crocheted the table centre, I cross stitched the tea-cosy pattern. I was at the time designing for machine-knitted jumpers so I punched out part of the design – the squirrel and the leaf – and put them into a jumper. The designs are shown in Fig 108. Any charted design can be cross stitched, used in needlepoint tapestry, crocheted, knitted by hand or machine, and even used as a basis for motifs for computer games – a sign of the times! Fig 109 shows a simple chart for a cross stitched D and the same design punched for a knitting machine where, of course, it is shown in reverse.

Another boundary I crossed was to take some patchwork designs and plot them for cross stitch; being based on mathematical shapes they worked out quite logically (Figs 110–115). I worked out two sizes of grids which will divide for American Block designs. You can make them larger but they will take a long time to stitch. The patterns are inevitably complex; as they are very dense I have only plotted the grids and filled in one quarter. Turn them through 45° each time as you fill the gaps.

To design your own, plot out a square 41

crosses square. Now by dividing and subdividing you can develop your own design. You will quite naturally come upon some of the old favourites as they are the result of logical mathematical progression, but you will also produce some that are your own.

The nine patch is an obvious one, but you can make it more personal by the types of filling patterns used to fill the squares, and the colours chosen. Try adding a bead or sequin here and there to make your work sparkle.

Perforated paper was a great favourite with the Victorians. I have a nineteenth-century example 'God blesseth the habitation of the Just', very moral but the shading used is quite lovely. It was used for cards as well. The paper is expensive to buy but you can make a lot from one sheet as you will have seen in the small projects in Chapter 6. However, the paper does damage easily so avoid mistakes.

Designs from mosaics and carpets are an excellent source of inspiration, for they too are based on a mathematical grid. While visiting a stately home I studied the carpet designs and produced the cross stitched piece shown in colour in the centre of page 93 and in Fig 116. The choice of colour is significant – the plum and turquoise vibrate together while the sage green unified the whole design. Some mosaics can be interpreted by freehand drawing and tracing them onto transparent graph paper. This is not a creative way to work but in some circumstances where you are preserving an idea that might otherwise be lost, it is permissible.

Fig 108 Charted designs
suitable for working in
cross stitch, crochet or
machine knitting

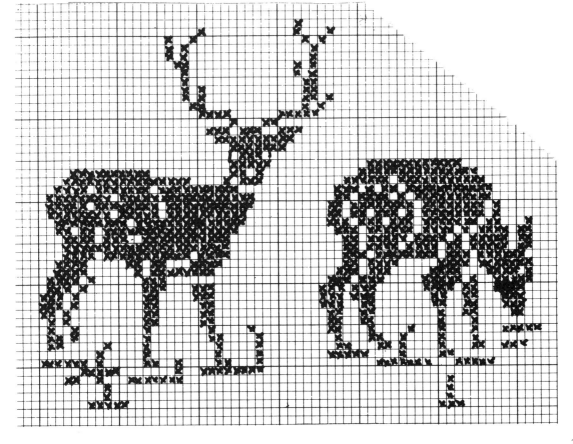

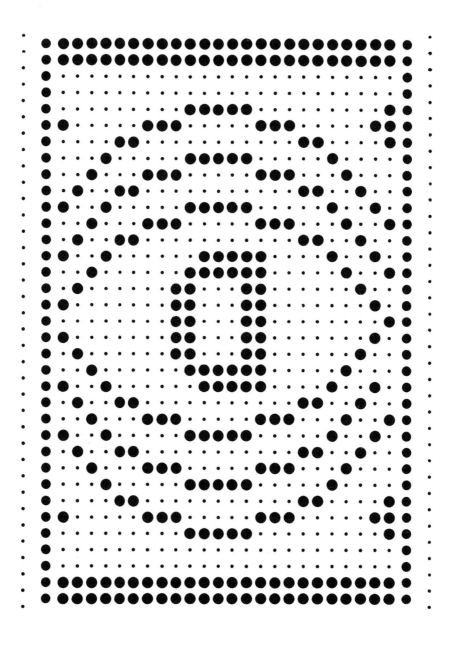

Fig 109 Chart for cross stitch D with punched card for same design for knitting machine, where it has to be reversed

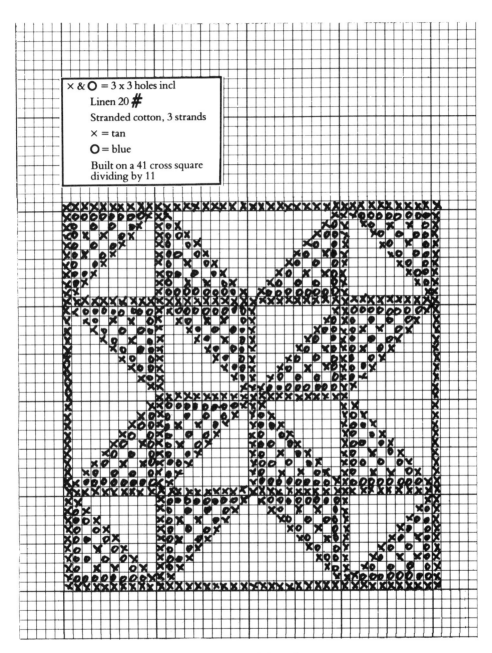

Fig 110 Rob Peter to Pay Paul; stitch the grid first, then infill

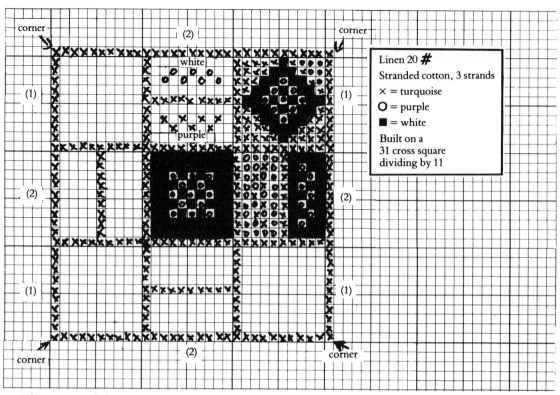

Fig 111 Johnnie Round the Corner; very complicated to plot – repeat sections 1 and 2 where indicated to completely fill the design

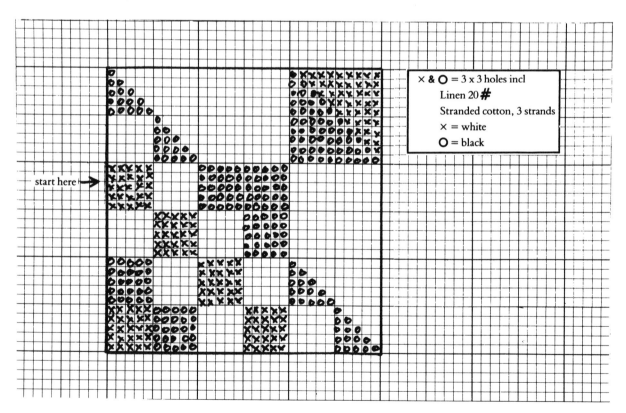

Fig 112 Steps to the Altar; worked in blocks of crosses, then outlined with double running stitch

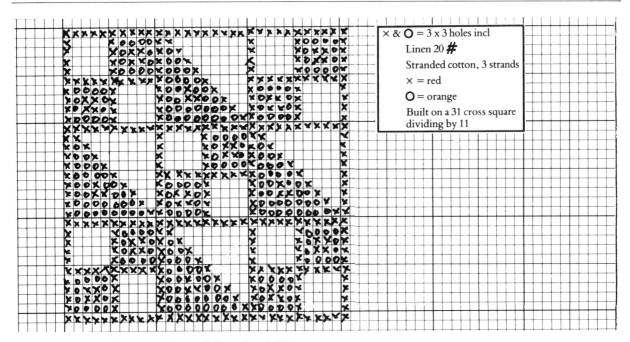

Fig 113 Jacob's Ladder; work the grid first, then infill

Fig 114 Author's variation on Corner Posts; the centre infill has crosses with running stitches around them to emphasise the diamond effect, worked in purple and brown with lavender vertical and horizontal running threads

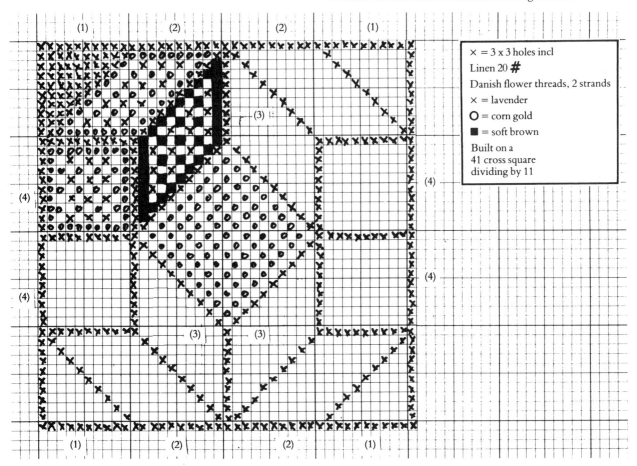

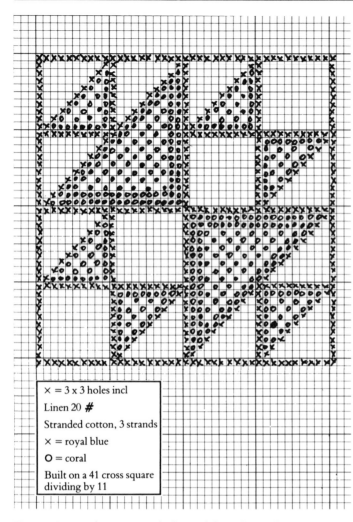

Fig 115 Fox and Geese; work the grid first, then infill

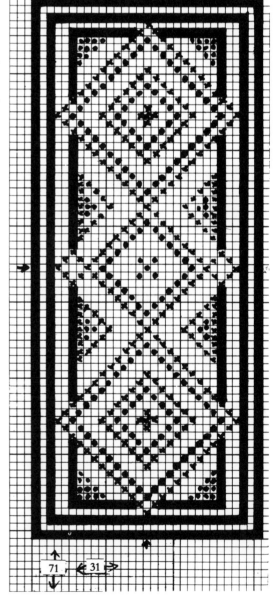

Fig 116 Cross stitch pattern based on a carpet design

9
A Year's Work

I thought it might be interesting for the reader to see gathered together the projects I have worked on during one year, to see how different ideas have been developed and how one idea can lead to another. The year began with my husband being involved with the local Gilbert & Sullivan group who were performing *The Mikado*. As it was the centenary year for this opera it seemed appropriate to stitch a piece (Fig 117).

I decided to divide up the design by a diagonal line of fans with the word 'Mikado' spelled out in them. I looked at various lines from the show and finally decided upon 'For he's going to marry Yum Yum' stitched in tiny script, with the three little maids stitched to follow the line of the fans. 'The flowers that bloom in the Spring' are above them. To the left of the fans is Tit Willow and in larger script 'And all is right as right can be'. The whole is enclosed by a zigzag border. The fabric is hardanger worked with stranded cottons in red, black, green, yellow and blue.

Much of the work done in 1985 was following a train of thought on the theme of flower gardens. Leading on from the ideas of taking patchwork into cross stitch, I began to look at formal gardens. Elizabethan knot gardens rely on the division of a square or rectangle in a symmetrical pattern. These were usually planted with box hedging to outline the shape and other flowers or herbs were planted in the gaps to make the pattern.

I began with a square of 39 crosses, this being the inner square. This was divided up with diagonal lines forming a cross. The heart shape, used here as a petal, outlined each one. Those were then filled and the corners stitched in green

to give the effect of leaves. The outer border is a double line of stitches with alternating colours from the flowers used to balance the design (Fig 118).

From this developed a larger piece using four squares, each one showing a different petal formation. The colours reflect the summer hues. Again the borders were filled with a sequential pattern using all the colours (Fig 119).

From this point I went off in two directions. The first was to explore the narrow border idea (Fig 120). The example of using it in a spiral formation gives a maze effect with a star at the centre (Fig 121). I also worked one with a picture frame idea of squares within squares and in the centre this time I put the yoga chant 'OM' (Fig 122). Then I combined a quote from a poem with a broken square with the sun in the centre and snowdrops at the corner (Fig 123).

The second area developed was to experiment with the flower head designs trying them as a repeat design, and from there to use this idea in a larger square with flowers rotating round the square (Fig 124). Then I tried out two 'rose' centres with different leaf surrounds (Figs 125 and 126). Again the narrow border is used to frame the piece.

The year 1985 was the Year of the Garden, so that was an obvious theme to think about. I decided to use a Latin phrase as it is shorter to stitch, and so 'Gloria Horti' came about (Fig 127). I wanted to develop further the narrow border theme and made the shape one of regular pathways. It is very formal with each space filled with a flower repeat while the narrow border inside frames the lettering. It is stitched on cotton evenweave in green, pink, blue and

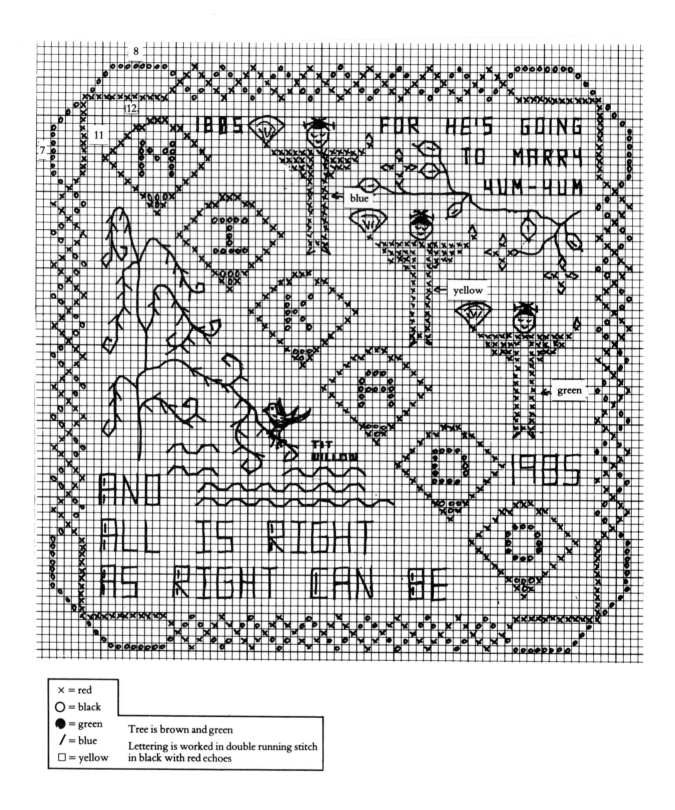

Fig 117 'The Mikado' celebration chart

Fig 118 Herb garden based on Elizabethan knot garden

purple stranded cottons. The design was 63 crosses square. I tried out the basic pattern on a sample before embarking on the finished piece.

Another Latin phrase stitched this year was 'Est Natus Hodie' meaning 'He is born today' – out of season, in fact, as I was experimenting with a combination of the star borders in Chapter 3 (Fig 128). I wanted to stitch it in black

with gold thread highlights, so it is worked on fine cotton evenweave stitched in silk with gold thread. It measures 77 crosses wide by 35 crosses high. See also Fig 41 in Chapter 3.

I felt I needed a change from all the intricate borders and squares, so at Easter I designed the egg shown on the dust jacket of the book (Fig 129). It was quite difficult to organise the outer

Fig 119 Flower garden

shape – in fact it was easier to stitch than to chart. I decided to put in lines to subdivide the egg and fill them with different patterns. I used a colour sequence with all the colours used in the centre panel. The humour comes in the form of a tiny chick coming from the large egg.

Another idea would be to divide the egg in the middle along the zigzag and put the chick in there. I worked with all the primary colours but it would also look attractive worked in shades of one colour. Again fine cotton was used with

stranded cotton thread. It measures 70 crosses wide by 84 crosses high.

During the summer of 1985 while on holiday in Yorkshire, I came across a motif that appealed to me. I had no graph paper with me at the time and so have worked from memory so I expect that it is nothing like the original. We visited Whitby and I saw the motto in cast iron on the bridge – again in Latin. Fuimus, Sumus (We were, we are). I added Erimus (we will be) and plotted out this design using my adaptation

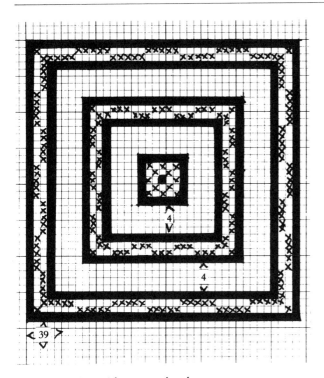

Fig 120 Design with narrow borders

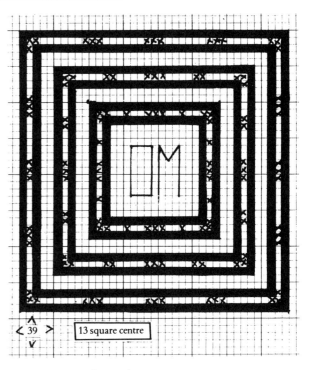

Fig 122 Picture frame theme

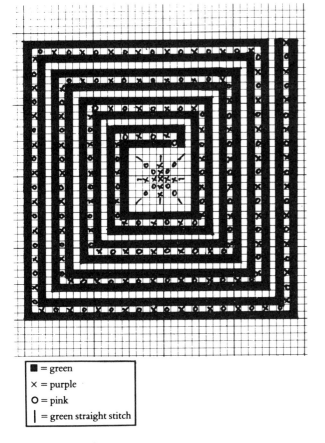

■ = green
× = purple
O = pink
| = green straight stitch

Fig 121 Maze theme

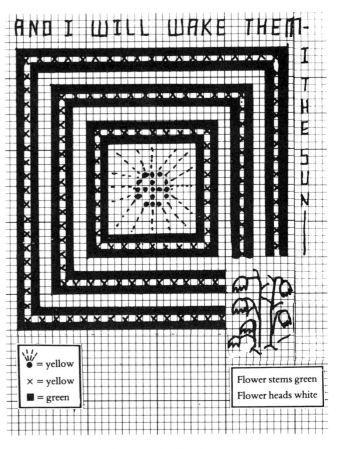

●̈ = yellow
× = yellow
■ = green

Flower stems green
Flower heads white

Fig 123 Extension of narrow border theme

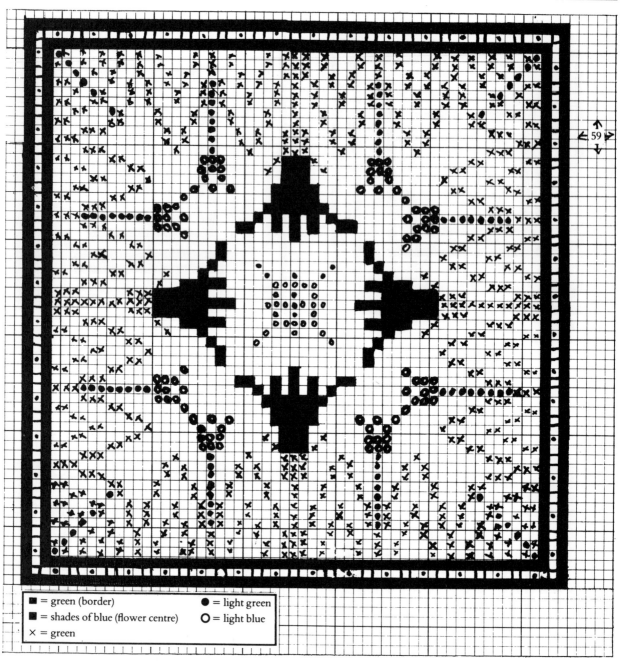

Fig 124 Design to suggest bluebells or fuchsias

Legend:
- ■ = green (border)
- ■ = shades of blue (flower centre)
- × = green
- ● = light green
- O = light blue

of the border I saw – a holiday memento (Fig 130). I have plotted several variations of the border to show how it changes (Fig 131).

During that holiday I repeatedly saw examples of the White Rose of York, and worked on my own simple interpretation (Fig 132).

I came back from Yorkshire with an idea about showing the growth of York from early times. Having visited Jorvik, the remarkable reconstruction of Viking York, I felt I wanted to depict the important influences of the past. I have played around with the previous names for the city and intend to use patterns relevant to each period and, where possible, to stitch in colours prevailing at each time. Fig 133 shows my preliminary ideas – there is much still to be done . . .

Other pieces I stitched during the year have fallen naturally into earlier chapters. These include 'Summer', Fig 79 in Chapter 5 which is a

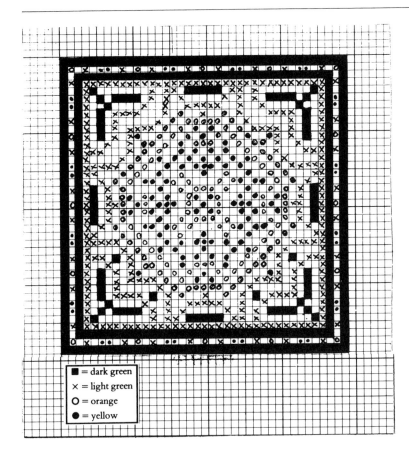

= dark green
= light green
= orange
= yellow

Fig 125 Rose garden with leafy surround

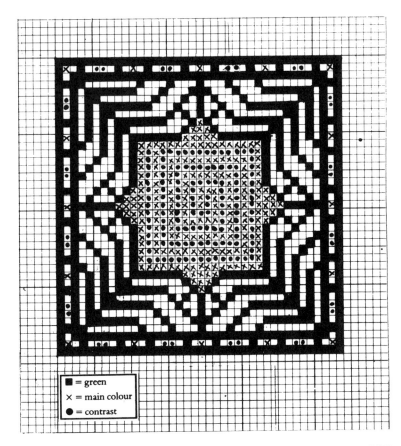

= green
= main colour
= contrast

Fig 126 Rose garden combined with maze theme

137

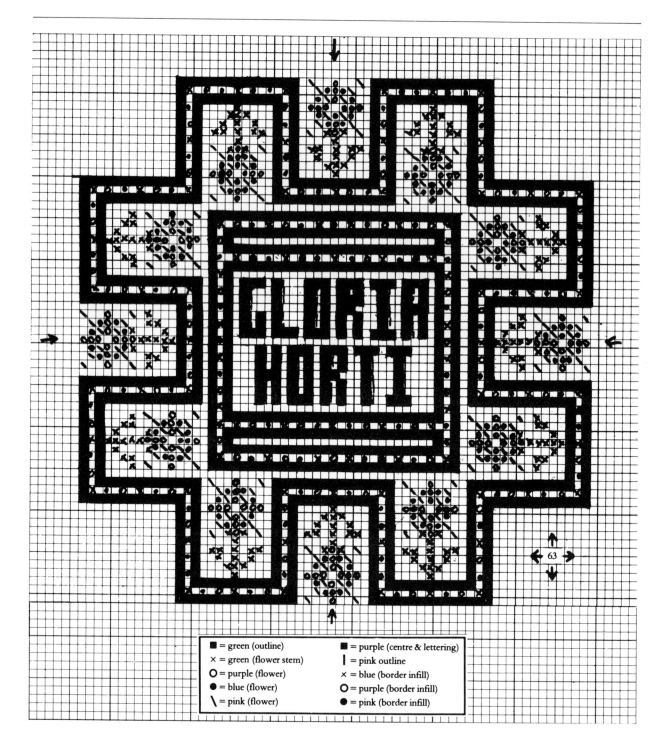

Fig 127 'The glory of the garden' – designed to celebrate 1985 as the Year of the Garden

simple interpretation of the garden theme; 'The Way to My Heart', Fig 89 in Chapter 5 which develops the maze concept; some of the patchwork interpretations in Chapter 8 and particularly Fig 116, based on a carpet design seen on holiday, whose outer rectangular border is now very familiar, but with an active middle pattern which breaks beyond the confines of the inner border.

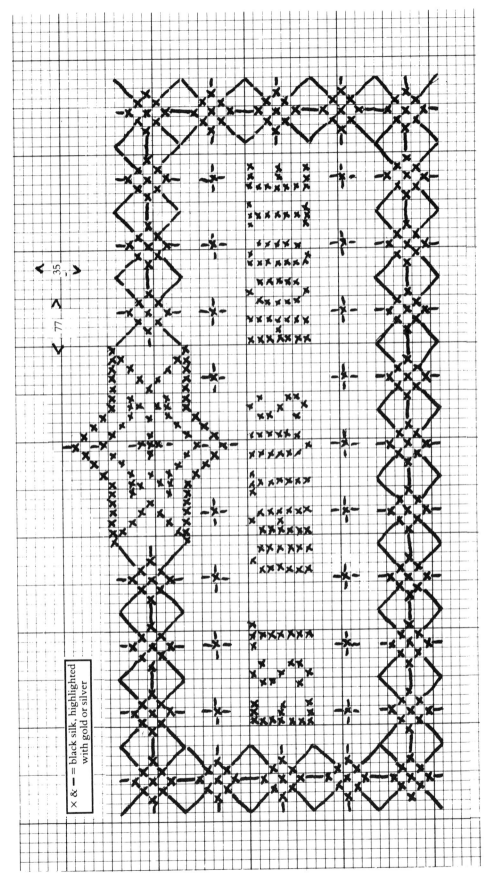

Fig 128 A variation on the star border in Fig 41

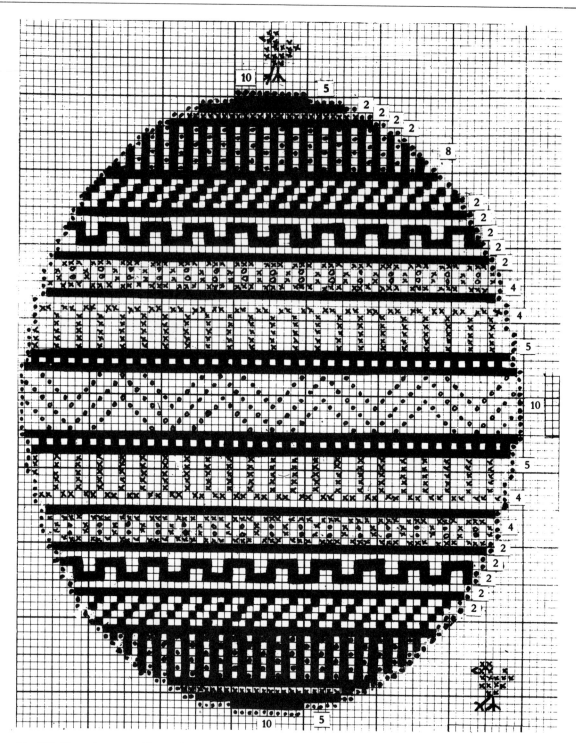

Fig 129 Chart for cover illustration

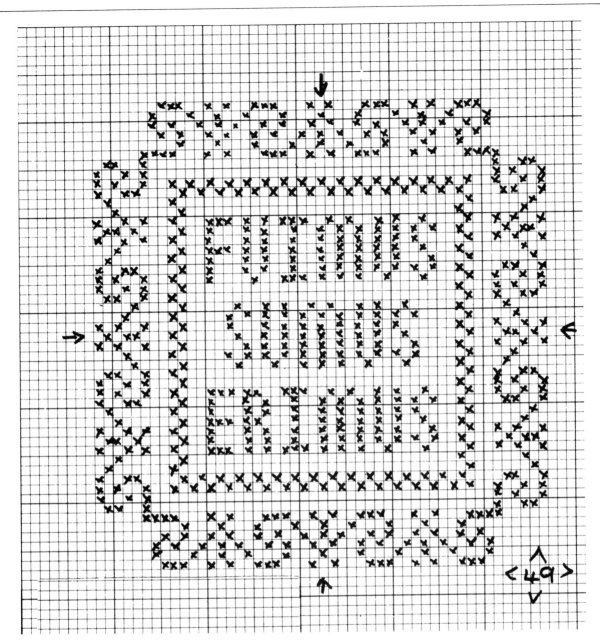

Fig 130 Part of motto taken from bridge in Whitby, North Yorkshire, with a border interpreted from a sampler in York Museum

Conclusion

Looking back over the years that this book spans I hope you will see a development in style and technique. Learning is never static; it is a lifelong process and leads you down many avenues that you have never thought about. I hope this book will help the readers to be stimulated to try designing for themselves and to gain as much satisfaction and pleasure from their work as I have had.

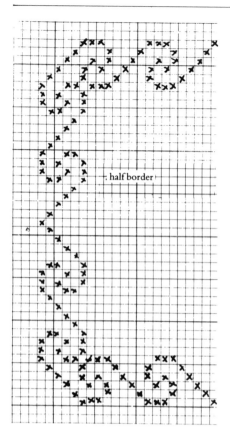

: half border :

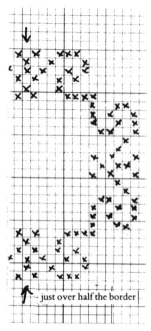

just over half the border

Fig 131 Variations on the border in Fig 130

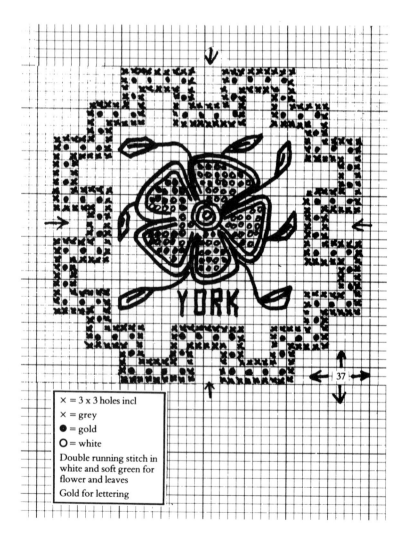

× = 3 x 3 holes incl

× = grey

● = gold

○ = white

Double running stitch in white and soft green for flower and leaves

Gold for lettering

Fig 132 The author's interpretation of the White Rose of York

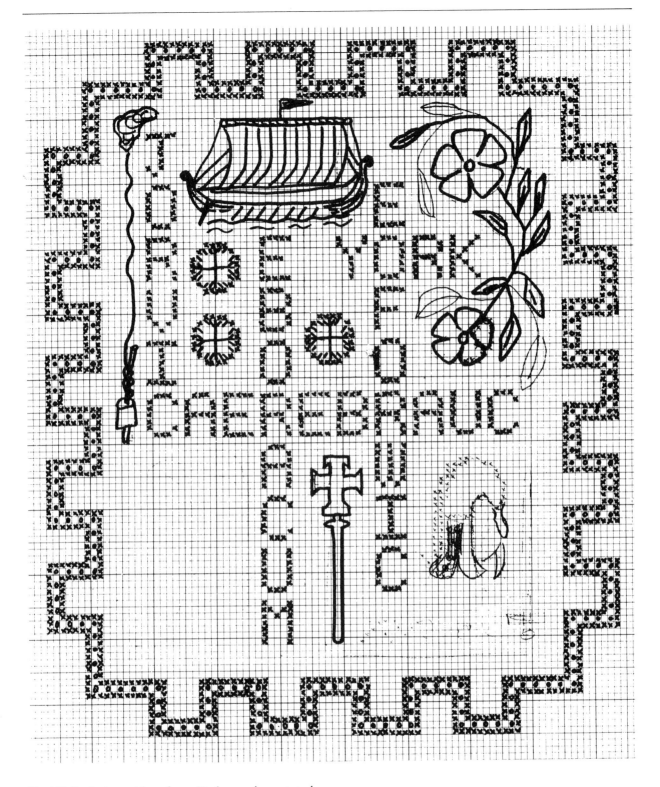

Fig 133 Preliminary ideas for a York sampler, yet to be finished

Index